WOOD CRAFT

WOOD CRAFT

MASTER THE ART OF
GREEN WOODWORKING

Penguin Random House

Contributors Robin Duckmanton,
Tom Hepworth, Sophie Ridley,
Harry Samuel, Tim Sanderson

Senior Editor Alastair Laing

Senior Designer Collette Sadler

Editorial Assistant Megan Lea

Design Assistant India Wilson

Managing Editor Dawn Henderson

Managing Art Editor Marianne Markham

Jacket Designer Steve Marsden

Senior Producer (Pre-Production)
Tony Phipps

Senior Producer Luca Bazzoli

CTS Sonia Charbonnier

Art Director Maxine Pedliham

Publishing Director Mary-Clare Jerram

Photographer Mark Winwood

Illustrator Andrew Torrens

First published in Great Britain in 2019
by Dorling Kindersley Limited
One Embassy Gardens, 8 Viaduct Gardens, London, SW11 7BW

Copyright © 2019 Dorling Kindersley Limited
A Penguin Random House Company
10 9 8 7 6 5 4 3
005–310526–May/2019

Disclaimer: see p256

A CIP catalogue record for this book
is available from the British Library.
ISBN: 978-0-2413-4379-1

Printed and bound in China

A WORLD OF IDEAS:
SEE ALL THERE IS TO KNOW
www.dk.com

Contents

WHAT IS
WOOD CRAFT?

Wood craft is woodwork at a human level. It relies, for the most part, upon humble folk traditions rather than machines. Using simple hand tools, perfected over millennia, keeps you close to the material and leads to a far more rewarding experience.

Crafting objects by hand engenders a close relationship with the products – spending time making an everyday item such as a spoon really helps you to appreciate its form and function. By choosing to craft objects that you will use day in, day out, you are challenged to confront their functionality and their beauty.

Wood craft also describes a more holistic approach to wood. Being in close contact with living trees, perhaps understanding them as sources of fuel or food, contributes to a wider understanding of wood culture.

In this book we have used hand tools where possible. Working in this way, you can practise your craft almost anywhere without the need to plug into an electrical socket, and because there is less noise and dust, it can work socially. All over the world there are local spoon clubs, where groups sit around and carve together – what could be more natural than that? Crafting helps you develop a relationship

with the environment, and it can give you a different concept of existence, away from the two-dimensional world of smartphone screens. Beliefs gained from wood craft are practical and philosophical: that it is better to use abrasives for sharpening tools, rather than fixing the rough surface created by blunt ones; that wood is often better cleft than sawn; and that empathy for the tools and material makes for better products.

"But why should I bother making these things when they can be bought so cheaply?" you may ask. Put simply, mass-produced items do not serve all of our needs. Whether buying the crafts of others or making objects for loved ones, the human condition finds something in craft that is not found in modern consumerism.

We have chosen projects that teach core skills and the key properties of the material. We hope that they will inform and inspire. In wood craft, much of the joy of creating comes from interaction with the wood fibres and seeing where the material takes back control of the shape, and how to work with that. By exploring the properties of wood, working with them to enhance the effectiveness of a product, and learning how to alter the design to make up for where the material may be lacking, you will become a well-rounded maker.

> 66 IT IS **WIDELY** BELIEVED THAT **CRAFT** IS **GOOD** FOR YOU. 99

A woodworker *should know the shape of the leaves on the tree that the wood came from.*

WOOD

The first step in woodworking, as with any craft, is to get to grips with your material. Green woodworking in particular calls for fresh, unseasoned wood, which is therefore soft and pliable enough to be crafted with hand tools. The story begins with the tree.

The water content of freshly felled green wood varies between species, time of year, and other circumstances. A log can have more weight in water than from the wood itself. Once felled, and over time, this water leaves the wood until it reaches equilibrium with its environment. First to evaporate is the free water within transport fibres and cells; most shrinkage, however, occurs from the evaporation of water bound within the cellulose of cell walls. With experience, you gain a feel for when wood has dried out. When you need to be more precise, for example in joinery projects, you can weigh components to be sure: if they are kept in an airing cupboard and are no longer losing weight, they won't normally shrink any further.

These days, virtually all forestry is done with machines – often large harvesting machines as opposed to individuals with chainsaws. In the past, the management of forests and woodlands was done by hand, with more of the focus on coppicing, a traditional method of woodland management that yields smaller, more manageable products, and tends to be popular in cultures that rely on intensively managed wood.

> " IN THE **PAST**, THE MANAGEMENT OF **FORESTS** AND **WOODLANDS** WAS DONE BY HAND. "

A coppiced wood (also known as a copse) is an area of managed woodland that is cut on rotation, to create a useful renewable material. Groups of young trees are cut down to near ground level – the stumps that remain are called stools. Through monitoring and controlling the age a coppice stool grows to, it is possible to manage the size of the resulting product, which is often of great quality and knot free because of fast growth from the established stool.

Lifecycle of managed woodland

Managed woodlands are made up of stands – groups of trees in a specific area, usually of a similar age or size. Seedlings grow into saplings, which become poles when they grow beyond around 10cm (4in) in diameter. A single stem

Sustainably managed *diverse woodland can provide perfect materials for wood craft.*

tree within a stand or a copse is often called a standard; usually, a minimum of 20 years is required for that standard to become worth turning into firewood and timber.

After 60 years of growth, a tree will usually have a diameter of around 30cm (12in). Hardwoods and saw logs from timber trees start at around 50cm (20in) in diameter. A 20-year-old copse grown for firewood and timber may include standards that would be grown on to reach larger diameters, traditionally for timber frames. Traditionally, each time a rotation came around, decisions would have to be made by those managing the wood about what to do with the standards – whether they should become part of the copse, or be grown on.

Even when it is not a coppice wood, managed woodland tends to be planted very close together, to encourage competitive growth.

> 66 THERE IS A SIGNIFICANT DIFFERENCE IN THE QUALITY OF FAST-GROWN WOOD COMPARED TO SLOW-GROWN. 99

After 20 years, it is thinned out, leaving only the stronger trees – this process is often done in several stages. In intensive forestry, trees may also be pruned, to produce knot-free boards.

Growth rates

A young tree will increase its growth rate each year until it plateaus and then declines. It will continue to increase in size, but at a slower rate.

For both economical and environmental reasons, it makes sense to harvest stands when their growth rate starts to decline. Trees take the most carbon dioxide out of the atmosphere when they are growing fastest, and, when cut on rotation and managed for diversity, a useful crop can also create a fantastic habitat for wildlife.

Thinner rings do not necessarily mean less growth: the circumference of the ring has to increase with each year, so the rate of growth may be increasing though the width of the ring remains the same or even decreases.

There is a significant difference in the quality of fast-grown wood compared to slow-grown. Fast-grown wood is much stronger, particularly in terms of its tensile strength, and also denser, especially when dry. Slow-grown wood includes that found on the outer growth rings of large trees that are competing with others in the canopy. It can be lovely to carve, and often perfectly strong enough for many uses.

Heartwood *is formed of xylem, which conducts water around the tree*

Sapwood *is also formed of xylem, but, unlike heartwood, sapwood is still active*

Inner bark (bast) *is formed of phloem, which conducts sugars around the tree*

Outer bark *is known as cork cambium*

GROWTH RINGS

Cambium
growth layer

Latewood
– vessels have smaller diameters

Earlywood
– vessels have larger diameters

RING-POROUS WOOD

Wood anatomy
New wood grows in rings between layers of existing wood, which is often comprised of the heartwood, in the centre, and sapwood, closer to the edge.

New wood

Wood is largely made up of cellulose and lignin. Cellulose provides tensile strength, and lignin offers compressional strength. Softwoods have higher lignin content than hardwoods. New wood grows between layers of existing wood (*see* Wood anatomy, above).

In species that form distinct growth rings, there are three fundamental patterns of earlywood and latewood:
- No change in cell type across the growth ring.
- A gradual reduction of the inner diameter of conducting cells from the earlywood to the latewood.
- Abrupt and distinct change in the inner diameter of conducting cells from the earlywood to the latewood.

Ring-porous wood has more vessels of larger diameter in the spring (early) growth compared to the summer (late) growth, making the rings very distinct from each other (*see* Ring-porous wood illustration, above).

In conifers, late growth is denser and remains relatively constant, whereas early growth reduces. The slow growth rate, or smaller width of growth rings, means softwoods with more rings per inch are stronger. I would recommend softer woods for carving as greater tensile strength is often not required. However, this is not the case with furniture or the frame saw, which may need to be significantly bulkier if wood with a high tensile strength isn't used.

Plank

A coat peg *can be fashioned from a branch – see p64*

Making the most of the material
The possibilities hidden in the tree are nearly endless. Consider the grain carefully when planning projects, to make the best use of the material. And keep in mind that knots tend to occur in the centre of wide logs.

The rounded outer side *can become the hollow of a bowl – see p82*

Stool legs *can be made from this straight-grained billet – see p130*

Curved grain *at the crook of a tree makes a perfect spoon – see p70*

Interlocked fibres *near the base give the wood strength – ideal material for the steep end-grain walls of a "kuksa" drinking cup*

A full-length plank *taken from the centre of a tree tends to split along the pith*

FROM TREE TO PROJECT

Sourcing green wood

Methods of finding or buying wood vary depending on where you live, and what sort of resources are available to you, but below are a few pointers. Bear in mind that trees grown in woodlands tend to be straighter than city or park trees and have fewer knots, because they are competing against the canopy, so strive to grow upwards, without many side branches.

■ Woodland is often managed by conservationists, who may remove invasive species of tree or introduce new ones to support wildlife and diversity. Contact conservationists in your area to see if they will supply wood from their management operations.

■ Firewood merchants are also a useful resource – ideally, you should get the wood before it has been sawn and split; it will often have been left in the forest for some time before being collected by a firewood merchant, but it is usually still green.

■ Find out who manages the trees in your local parks or cemeteries, and ask if any spare wood is available.

■ In non-urban areas, foresters and coppice workers are your best bet. In towns and cities, park wardens are often more useful than tree surgeons, who tend to work on difficult trees – foreign or unusual species that have been planted in gardens, or trees that are diseased. To protect buildings from possible damage caused by felling larger lengths, trees in cities are usually ringed. This means that the wood dries much more quickly, and is often wasted, though wood

66 TREES GROWN IN WOODLAND TEND TO BE STRAIGHTER THAN CITY OR PARK TREES. 99

found in this way can be very useful.

■ For boards, a timber yard is your best bet. Look for a timber specialist who takes their time and allows you to identify the best boards – hopefully not at the bottom of the stack!

Buying blanks

You can buy cleft and sawn blanks (pieces of wood ready for carving) online from reputable suppliers, so that you know they are responsibly sourced and have the correct grain alignment and moisture content.

Storing green wood

Before buying or gathering your wood, make sure you have adequate space to store it. Small pieces of wood will remain green if kept in bags of damp shavings; avoid storing in this way for too long, as the sugars can encourage moulds. Small pieces can also be kept in the freezer to keep them green. Keep larger logs green by sealing the ends with paint wax or PVA glue.

CHAPTER 01

KNIFEWORK

Baton a log or use a ready-made blank and start crafting. With a straight knife as your principal tool, work through this chapter to create practical objects and perfect key knife grips.

MAKE A
BUTTER SPREADER

This wooden spreader has a wide paddle and is very light to handle: once you try it, you will never go back to metal. A spreader makes the perfect first project for learning knife skills, as the wood fibres are aligned in one flat plane, which allows you to focus on carving in the correct direction around the profile shape.

You will need

TOOLS & EQUIPMENT
- Pencil
- Measuring equipment
- Straight knife
- Mallet-sized log or mallet
- *optional:* Axe

MATERIALS
- 1 green wood log, around 75mm (3in) in diameter and 180mm (7in) in length

Skills

YOU WILL LEARN TO
- Baton (split) wood with a knife: *steps 1–2*
- Carve with a knife: *steps 3–6*
- Carve a chamfered edge: *steps 7–8, 11*

KNIFE GRIPS
- Chest lever: *p19*
- Thumb pull: *p21*
- Thumb push, pivot: *p22*

Design guide

When carving an object it can be useful to follow a specific order of carving stages to home in on the final shape. For the spreader, start by tapering the billet towards the paddle end, thinning from both sides but leaving thickness in the handle for comfort. From there, proceed to shape the profile, following the stages numbered below.

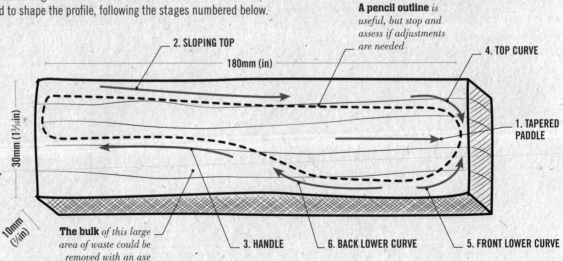

2. SLOPING TOP

A pencil outline is useful, but stop and assess if adjustments are needed

4. TOP CURVE

180mm (in)

30mm (1³⁄₁₆in)

1. TAPERED PADDLE

10mm (⁵⁄₈in)

The bulk *of this large area of waste could be removed with an axe*

3. HANDLE

6. BACK LOWER CURVE

5. FRONT LOWER CURVE

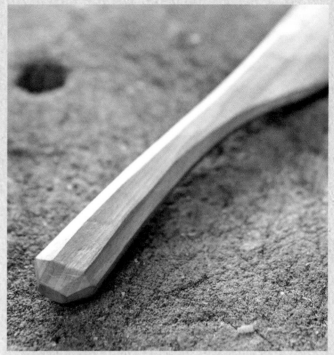

> 66 THE SPREADING ACTION
> OF A WOODEN PADDLE
> CANNOT BE BEATEN. 99

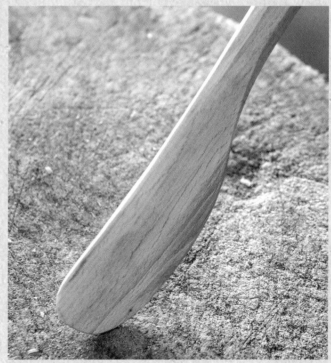

FOCUS ON...
RUNNING OFF

If you try to split off a thin billet from a thicker piece, the split will often "run off" towards the edge of the thin blank, where fibres are under greater tension. This is why it tends to be better to split sections of wood in half and then half again until you end up with the correct size.

A split started *in the middle is more likely to run straight*

Splits nearer the edge *tend to run off to the thinner part*

The Process

1 Split the log
First split – or "baton" – the log in half and then half again with a knife. Make the initial split by firmly tapping on the spine of the knife with a small mallet or suitable piece of wood. Once the blade is fully embedded, continue by tapping down on the protruding point of the knife to chase the split right through the log.

Use gentle force *to tap the knife down the length of the log, which should split along the grain*

2 Baton out a blank
You are aiming to take a full width plank from the side of a quartered log. To reduce the risk of running off (*see above*), first split the quarter in two, making sure what's left is large enough that when split in two again you have a little plank around 10mm (⅜in) thick; this will be your carving piece, or "blank". Wood split along the radius of the log in this way – called "radial" – is less likely to cup (*see p103*) as it dries because the grain is relatively straight.

3 Start on the paddle

As per the order of carving on p16, the first stage is to create the paddle taper by thinning down wood at one end, using the knife in chest lever grip; *see* above. Start to take shavings on the near side of the blank, from just under halfway along its length. Make an angled cut that takes off the corner of the blank edge, to create a "facet". Then cut another facet that takes off the corners of the first. The process of whittling is, in essence, cutting a series of facets that take off corners and high points.

4 Taper the paddle

Continue cutting facets across the width of the blank, then turn it over and cut the same facets on the other side. Regularly turn the blank over as you whittle, to take off even amounts of wood on both sides. Take off more material as you progress towards the end of the blank, so that you create a tapering profile to a thin end of about 2mm (1/16in).

Engage the blade *near the tip to make cuts to the far side of the blank*

CONTINUED ☞

TIP

For speed, you could remove the substantial amount of waste wood under the handle with an axe; *see* Shaping with an axe, p50.

Make shallow *cuts for fine shaping*

5 Shape the sloping top

Still using chest lever grip, make cuts along one of the long edges of the blank to form the profile of the top of the spreader. You are aiming to shape a shallow concave that descends from the handle end and rises slightly as it approaches the paddle end.

You will see *the basic shape of the spreader start to take form*

6 Shape the handle

Holding the blank at the paddle end, form a handle around 15mm (⁹⁄₁₆in) wide by removing waste from the base side. Still in chest lever grip, start cuts from just under halfway along the blank, from what will be the start of the paddle. Cut a concave that starts fairly steeply and then levels out for the handle shaft, before rising again slightly at the handle end.

1. Hold the knife in your fingertips, with your index finger high up on the handle and your palm open and empty.

2. Close your fingers on to your palm. Keep your thumb out of the direction of the cut by positioning it at 10 o'clock to the blade's 12 o'clock; or at 2 o'clock if you are left-handed.

7 Facet the handle and paddle

Before moving on to the paddle, create a more rounded shape to the handle by cutting a series of eight facets down its length, shaving off the corners all round to form a squashed octagon shape when seen in cross-section. Turn the blank around and continue the same series of facets to round off the corners of the paddle.

Aim to cut *single long shavings for a smooth finish*

8 Chamfer the handle

Now neaten the end of the handle by cutting a 45° bevel all round – known as a "chamfer" – using the thumb pull grip; *see* above. Chamfering not only gives a neat appearance, but by taking off square edges it also makes surfaces more comfortable to grip.

Position your thumb *so that it is offset from the blade as you squeeze the grip*

CONTINUED ☞

THUMB PUSH & PIVOT GRIPS

1. For thumb push, place your clenched thumb level with where you want to start the cut. Put your thumb on the back of the knife, in the middle offset from the tip, which makes the cut engage the blade. Push it forwards by extending your thumb.

2. For thumb pivot, instead of pushing with your thumb, keep it still so that it acts as a pivot for the cutting movement made by the wrist of your other hand.

Shape a long curve *at the base and a shorter, shallower curve at the top*

9 Curve the paddle

Use thumb push grip to cut the curved shape of the paddle; *see* above. Curve the top of the paddle first, then the lower curve at the front, followed by the lower curve at the back as it blends into the handle. Don't attempt to cut curves in one or two deep shavings. Knock off a corner first, then shave off the corners of this first cut, and so on; as the curve starts to form, you can take off longer shavings.

10 Dress the surface

Create a smooth finish to – or "dress" – the flat faces of the paddle. Employ thumb push grip for an initial tidy-up, then switch to thumb pivot grip for finer cuts; *see* above.

Remove any *rough patches, high points and nicks*

Design variations

While staying in the same flat plane, play around with shape and scale to create other useful kitchen utensils. Build in functionality by thinking hard about what jobs the utensil will be called on to do.

SPATULA

Optional hole *can be drilled and chamfered, for hanging on a hook*

Wide chamfer *cut into the paddle edge for flipping food*

JAM SPREADER

Pointed end *to the paddle for scraping in the corners of jars*

Steep "crank", *or mid-section, to help with the scooping action*

11 Round off edges
Finally, return to thumb push grip and cut a chamfer along the edges of the butter spreader paddle (the handle has already been chamfered), to remove sharp edges and create a comfortable, neat finish.

Take long, *thin shavings for a neat chamfered edge*

MAKE A

TOGGLE

Carving a toggle is a fantastic way to improvise a simple and effective fastener. They can be used in a variety of ways; in conjunction with short loops of material for a button fixing on a duffle coat, for example, or for drawing through and knotting off a length of cord to open and close a bag.

YOU WILL NEED

TOOLS AND EQUIPMENT
- Bench hook
- Handsaw (such as a pull saw)
- Straight knife
- Small mallet
- Electric drill

MATERIALS
- A branch, around 30mm (1³⁄₁₆in) in diameter and at least 64mm (2½in) long, but longer is convenient to hold and allows for multiple toggles
- Cord

SKILLS

YOU WILL LEARN TO
- Cut with a pull saw: *step 6*
- Use an electric drill: *step 2*

REMIND YOURSELF HOW TO
- Baton (split) wood with a knife: *p16*
- Carve with a knife: *p16*
- Carve a chamfered edge: *p16*

KNIFE GRIPS
- Chest lever: *p19*
- Thumb pivot: *p22*

DESIGN GUIDE

The lozenge-like horizontal design creates a sturdy toggle, strong without being too cumbersome. The tapered ends enable it to be used like a handle and easily slip through a loop or button hole; they also make the toggle comfortable to hold and introduce a pleasing curvature to the aesthetic.

Notch provides *recess so cord can sit flush when loose*

1. FACETED MAIN BODY

60mm (2³⁄₈in)

Ends given *a chamfered point*

19mm (³⁄₄in)

4. CHAMFERED ENDS

Holes drilled *to match the size of intended cord*

Sides taper mainly *along their width, only slightly in their depth*

3. TAPERED SIDES

OVERHEAD VIEW

2. RECESSED NOTCH

> "IMPROVING THE **FUNCTIONALITY** OF THREAD, CORDAGE, AND ROPE WITH THE **ADDITION** OF **WHITTLED** WOODEN ARTEFACTS IS AN **ANCIENT TECHNOLOGY**, AND NO LESS USEFUL TODAY."

USING A PULL SAW

Saw blades can jump when starting a cut, but the risk is greatly reduced once at least three teeth are in contact. To this end, start by drawing the blade in the opposite direction to the sawing action – with a pull saw, by pushing it – to gently create a slot for the teeth to rest in.

Rest your thumb on the top edge of the blade to steady and control initial cuts.

A bench hook provides space for cutting and an edge to work to, and enables you to hold the object steady.

The Process

1 Size the wood
Cut a section of wood from the branch with a pull saw (*see* above), leaving enough excess so that it is easy to grip when carving. Baton the section in half vertically with a knife.

Technique: Batoning with a knife – see p16

Aim to split
down the middle, through the pith

2 Drill holes
Drill a pair of holes through one of the halves. The diameter of drill bit depends on the thickness of cord: neither too loose nor so tight that it is difficult to thread. Ensure the holes are centred, about 19mm (¾in) from the edge, and try to drill straight down (but *see* Truing angled holes, above right). Minimise "tearout" by drilling through into some scrap wood.

TRUING ANGLED HOLES

Drilling holes exactly straight can be difficult. If your holes have ended up slanted, remedy the situation by truing to the angle of the holes. To do this, make cuts to the top and bottom of the toggle at such an angle that the faces end up perpendicular to the drilled holes.

Shave down *at an angle corresponding to the slant of the hole*

New faces *at top and bottom are now 90° to the hole*

Shave down *until the pith is no longer showing*

3 Smooth off

Turning to your knife, employ the chest lever grip to smooth off any tearout caused by drilling the holes. At the same time, remove the pith and some of the youngest growth wood with the tightest rings, which, if left in, make the toggle more prone to splitting.

Knife grip: Chest lever – see p19

Try to cut *single, long shavings for a smooth finish*

4 Facet the toggle

Still with chest lever, remove the bark and start shaping the toggle by cutting a series of facets down its length: two wide facets top and bottom, then six thinner facets connecting them, to create the curved sides – you are aiming for a squashed octagon shape in cross-section. If need be, "true" the toggle so that the holes are perfectly straight; *see* Truing angled holes, above.

CONTINUED ☞

Hold the sides of the knife as you would a pencil, resting the handle in the crook of your hand.

Make gentle cuts by moving the blade with finger and thumb, just as with writing. Keep everything steady: rest your hand on the bench and hold the toggle firmly.

Take care! Your fingers will be close to the sharp edge of the blade. Keep all fingers out of the direction of cut in case the knife slips.

5 Cut a notch

Holding the knife with pencil grip (*see* above), cut a shallow notch between the holes on one side of the toggle. Carve out the notch with the tip of the knife, resting the toggle on a work surface. The notch should be deep enough to allow the cord to sit flush when threaded.

Pull the cord
*tight to test the
notch depth*

6 Saw to size

Place the toggle on the bench hook and saw off the excess wood, ensuring the holes are centred in the toggle. The excess can be used to make further toggles.

> **THE JOY** OF MAKING FUNCTIONAL OBJECTS LIES IN THE **USING**. AS YOU **ENGAGE** WITH THE **DESIGN** YOU CAN **PERFECT** IT OVER TIME. **"**

Continue *the facets into the chamfers*

7 Taper and chamfer

Use chest lever grip to taper the toggle on both sides, which looks attractive and makes it easier to fit into button holes, if needed. Shave along the existing facets, and keep swapping sides and working both ends to ensure even tapers. Switch to thumb pivot grip to remove the square ends by cutting a chamfered finish.

Knife grip: Thumb pivot – see p22

Technique: Carving a chamfered edge – see p16

Design variations

The simplicity of toggles makes them endlessly adaptable. Folk craft often looks for ways to incorporate sculpture into functional pieces, such as with this fish-shaped light pull design.

BARREL TOGGLE

Profile is *streamlined with the cord*

Barrel shape *locates strength in the toggle's thickness*

FISH LIGHT PULL

Design inspired *by a fish caught on a hook and line*

Hole is wider *at the base for fitting a knot*

MAKE A
BANGLE

A wooden bangle is light and comfortable on the wrist. Wood grain can present some remarkable natural patterns, especially a section of highly figured spalted wood with dark lines left by fungal infection. Removing the central rings is an effective way to prevent the wood splitting as it dries.

YOU WILL NEED

TOOLS & EQUIPMENT
- Plywood
- Auger (or electric drill and frame saw)
- Straight knife
- Measuring equipment
- Pencil
- Mallet or mallet-sized log

MATERIALS
- Disk of green wood, around 100mm (3$\frac{15}{16}$in) in diameter and 30mm (1$\frac{3}{16}$in) thick (but be led by the wearer)

SKILLS

YOU WILL LEARN TO
- Use an auger: *step 1*
- Make circular cuts with a knife and produce rounded shaping: *steps 2, 5–7*
- Account for wood shrinkage: *step 3*

REMIND YOURSELF HOW TO
- Baton with a knife: *p16*

KNIFE GRIPS
- Reinforced pull: *p32*
- Chest lever: *p19*
- Thumb pull: *p21*

DESIGN GUIDE

The exact size of hole will be determined by the practicalities of fit, but personal choice can be exercised in the thickness and, to some degree, the shaping, depending on the style aimed for: chunky and bold, or sleek and elegant?

An oval shape *allows for the smallest bangle, since a hand can compress to an oval profile*

Centre the bangle *around the annular rings to ensure even shrinkage*

OVERHEAD VIEW

" BANGLES MUST BE CARVED WITH THE WEARER ALWAYS IN MIND. "

REINFORCED PULL GRIP

Grip the knife with the blade's tip vertical and your thumb resting on the blunt back. Be sure to stay clear of the protruding tip.

Reinforce the grip by clasping your cutting hand with your supporting hand.

Rotate the blade edge anti-clockwise around the interior surface (or rotate clockwise if you are left handed).

The Process

1 Cut the starter hole

Rest the disk on a spare bit of ply or other wood, to protect both the auger blade and the floor. Holding the disk steady with your feet, position the auger in the centre of the annular rings and turn the T-handle clockwise, all the time keeping it straight, until you've cut through.

2 Expand the hole

Use a knife to expand and shape the hole, employing the reinforced pull grip; *see* above. Don't try to take single cuts of the full circumference: stop when your wrist hits your chest and rotate the disk to take the next cut. If shaping an oval, take more material from two of the opposite quadrants.

Steady the disk *against your chest*

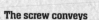
The screw conveys *wood shavings out of the hole as the auger turns*

TIP

If you don't have an auger, use an electric drill instead. You can also use a frame or coping saw to expand the hole.

Try drawing freehand *or join up a series of dots at the correct width*

3 Draw a guideline

Once happy with the size of hole, mark a pencil line for the width, parallel to the edge of the hole. Take account of shrinkage as the wood dries out: 10 per cent is a good rule of thumb; for example, if you are aiming for 90mm (3⁹⁄₁₆in) diameter, you should draw a line at 100mm (3¹⁵⁄₁₆in).

4 Baton to size

If the disk is significantly wider than the intended bangle, you can speed up the shaping process by batoning the wood roughly to size. Work round the disk, splitting off sections, but take care to leave enough waste around the guideline for fine shaping. At this point, leave the piece to dry for two weeks.

Technique: Batoning with a knife – see p16

Tap the point *of the knife with the mallet*

CONTINUED ☞

FOCUS ON...
RATES OF DRYING

Wood fibres dry at varied rates along the different axes. Removing central rings allows the wood to "move", hence avoiding splits that happen when the wood tries to change shape but can't without pulling itself apart.

Radial splits *occur because faster shrinkage on the tangent starts to pull the wood apart*

TANGENT 8%

RADIAL SPLITS

RADIUS 4%

Radial shrinkage *is half that of tangential*

LONGITUDE 0.3%

RATES OF SHRINKAGE

5 Shape the outside
Use chest lever grip to cut out the remaining waste and round off the exterior surface. Cut a series of three and then five even facets, in stages, around the circumference of the bangle, removing the corners between individual cuts and between facets to curve the surfaces.

Knife grip: Chest lever – see p19

Take off corners *of the first three facets to curve the surface*

6 Neaten the sides
Switch to the thumb pull grip to smooth off the rough sawn surface around the edge of the bangle, tidying up both sides. Keep your thumbs safely tucked away behind the bangle.

Knife grip: Thumb pull – see p21

> **CARVING THE ROUNDED SHAPE IS MADE EASIER BECAUSE YOU ARE NOT WORKING ACROSS THE END GRAIN.**

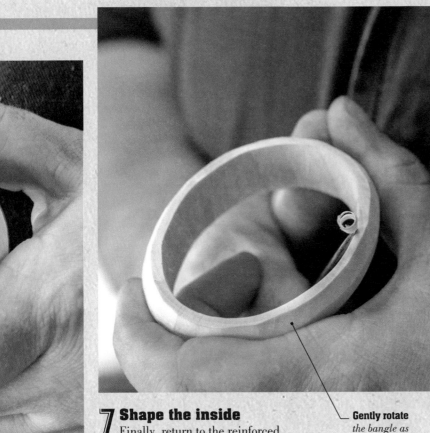

7 Shape the inside
Finally, return to the reinforced pull stroke to carve a convex surface on the inside of the bangle, rounding off the corners to mirror the five-faceted shape to the exterior of the bangle.

Gently rotate *the bangle as you make cuts*

Design variations
Once you have perfected carving a basic ring, you can get creative by adapting the size and exterior shape, and by introducing a taper, to produce different useful artefacts.

NAPKIN RING

A narrow hole *is better for clasping the napkin*

Experiment *with a more angular shape to the exterior*

EGG CUP

Hole size *will depend on the kind of eggs you like – hen, duck, or goose!*

Mimic the shape *of an egg by tapering to a wider top edge*

MAKE A
COFFEE PEG

This project makes use of the tensile strength and elastic properties of wood. Understanding these properties, and manipulating them to create an effective peg, will teach you many valuable lessons which can be taken forwards into other projects.

YOU WILL NEED

TOOLS & EQUIPMENT
- Electric drill and 15mm (⁹⁄₁₆in) drill bit
- Clamp
- Crosscut saw
- Straight knife

MATERIALS
- A green wood rod, around 38mm (1½in) in diameter and at least 150mm (5⅞in) in length, but a longer rod makes it far easier to saw in step 1

SKILLS

YOU WILL LEARN TO
- Make a "rip" cut: *step 1*
- Shape wood in order to make it flexible: *steps 3–7*

REMIND YOURSELF HOW TO
- Use an electric drill: *p24*
- Carve with a knife: *p16*
- Carve a chamfered edge: *p16*

KNIFE GRIPS
- Thumb pull: *p21*
- Reinforced pull: *p32*
- Forehand: *p39*
- Chest lever: *p19*
- Thumb pivot: *p22*

DESIGN GUIDE

The key practical issue with wooden pegs is that, with use, the split required to form the clasp has a natural tendency to continue up through the head of the peg. This design finds a simple and elegant solution to the problem by drilling a hole to spread the force of the split.

Thick chamfer *at the top of the peg*

38mm (1½in)

150mm (5⅞in)

Curved ends *facilitate flex and clipping*

Thin chamfer *around the bottom edges*

Deep side curves *facilitate flexing, while shallower curves on the faces maintain strength*

Tension-relieving hole *helps the peg to flex without splitting in half*

Bark retained *for rustic finish*

> 66 TIME WAS WHEN EVERY HOUSEHOLD WAS HOME TO WHITTLED OBJECTS. 99

FOCUS ON...
RELIEVING PRESSURE

If you were just to saw down the centre of the rod without having first drilled a hole, the peg would almost certainly split right down into two pieces during use. The hole spreads out the area where the splitting pressure is directed, meaning the top of the peg is much stronger, and won't need reinforcing.

Pressure from *the split is spread out by the hole*

HOLE PEG

All force *directed to a single point, causing split*

NON-HOLE PEG

The Process

1 Drill and saw the rod
Drill a hole through the centre of the rod 125mm (4$^{15}/_{16}$in) from an end. Clamp the rod to a work surface and saw vertically through the middle down to the hole. Sawing along the wood fibres like this is termed "ripping". Saw the rod off about 25mm (1in) beyond the hole.

Technique: Using an electric drill – see p24

— **To help sight** *the saw line, leave the drill bit in the hole as a guide*

2 Chamfer the top and peel off the bark
Switching to knifework, employ thumb pull grip to cut a neat chamfer at the top of the peg. Then remove most of the bark using mainly the reinforced grip, pivoting your wrist to make cuts. Leave a strip of bark between the chamfer and the hole. Switch to forehand grip to remove bark at the ends; *see* above right.

— **Cut a thick chamfer** *and shave off the sawn surface too*

Technique: Carving a chamfered edge – see p16

Knife grips: Thumb pull, Reinforced pull – see pp21, 32

Hold the wood in your non-dominant hand, across your thigh. Make a fist around the handle of the knife and point the blade diagonally upwards.

To make shavings, move the knife away from your body along the surface of the wood.

TIP
Cutting curves into the sides and faces enables the peg to flex along its length.

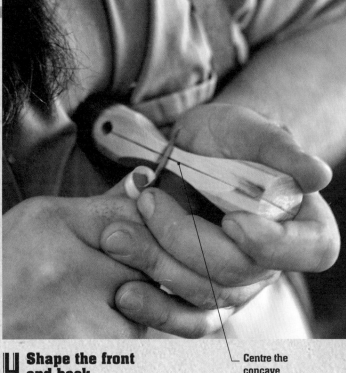

3 Shape the sides
Employ the reinforced grip to shape the outer parts of the peg, taking out the midsection of each side in a smooth curve, and leaving both ends at their full width. Carve from the end of the curve to the centre, then turn the peg around and carve in the same direction from the opposite end.

Take off thin *shavings, and ensure the peg ends up symmetrical*

4 Shape the front and back
In the same way, shave down the front and back faces of the peg, but do not shave too much off: create a more shallow concave than on the sides. Again, leave the ends at full thickness.

Centre the concave *at the midpoint of the peg, as with the sides*

CONTINUED ☞

TIP
With very wet wood, dab PVA glue on the top cut surface to slow drying and reduce risk of splits; carve off once fully dried.

> " AS YOU CARVE YOUR PEG, FOCUS ON CREATING SMOOTH LINES AND A SYMMETRICAL APPEARANCE. "

5 Shape inside the ends

Employ chest lever grip to remove material from inside the ends of the peg. Gradually work your way in and shape matching convex curves on both sides. Switch to thumb pivot grip to finesse the line of each curve.

Knife grips: Chest lever, thumb pivot – see pp19, 22

Begin the curve *around 19mm (¾in) from the end*

Blend the shape *of the ends into the curved sides and front and back faces*

6 Chamfer and shape the outsides

Remove the sharp edges at the ends by cutting a thin chamfer. Use a combination of thumb pivot grip for the sides and thumb pull for the very ends, to create a smooth edge. Switch to reinforced grip to remove material from the outsides of the ends, this time shaping concave lines parallel to the inside convex curves.

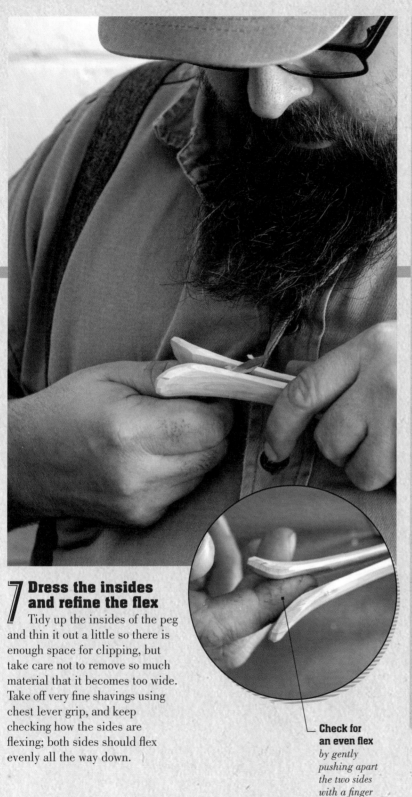

7 Dress the insides and refine the flex

Tidy up the insides of the peg and thin it out a little so there is enough space for clipping, but take care not to remove so much material that it becomes too wide. Take off very fine shavings using chest lever grip, and keep checking how the sides are flexing; both sides should flex evenly all the way down.

Check for an even flex *by gently pushing apart the two sides with a finger*

Design variations

Rather than trying to prevent the peg splitting, these alternative designs accept the likelihood of splitting and incorporate fixings to hold the two sides together.

GYPSY PEG

The split in *the peg runs all the way through it*

A thin strip of tin *pinned to the peg holds the two halves together*

PEGGED PEG

Peg fixing *is a smaller version of the type used for the Frame Stool, see p130*

Drill a hole 4.5mm (³/₁₆in) *wide for a 4mm (¹/₈in) peg*

MAKE A
PULLED FIBRE BRUSH

At its essence wood is a fibrous material, and this project offers a great way to explore and make use of this quality. As you form both the bristles of the brush and the woven binding holding them together, you are stretching the properties of the wood almost to breaking point, yet creating an object that is simple, functional, and beautiful.

YOU WILL NEED

TOOLS & EQUIPMENT
- Straight knife
- Small mallet
- *optional*: Handsaw (such as a pull saw)

MATERIALS
- 2 green wood rods, around 30mm ($^{13}/_{16}$in) in diameter; 300mm ($11^{13}/_{16}$in) long for the brush and 1000mm ($39^{3}/_{8}$in) long for the binding

SKILLS

YOU WILL LEARN TO
- Pull unbroken lengths of wood fibres: *steps 1–4*
- Split a rod down to a pliable strip: *steps 5–6*
- Weave with a wood strip: *step 7*

REMIND YOURSELF HOW TO
- Use a pull saw: *p24*
- Carve a chamfered edge: *p16*
- Baton with a knife: *p16*

KNIFE GRIPS
- Forehand: *p39*
- Thumb pull: *p21*

DESIGN GUIDE

The bristles of the brush are formed by pulling apart the wood into its constituent fibres. The central band of rod, left intact, acts as anchor to the fibres, enabling the rod to be stripped from both ends to create a thick head of bristles, leaving behind an ergonomic handle.

Fibres stripped
to leave handle

Chamfer cut
into handle end

Handle

Fibres fold
over to form brush head

SECOND SET OF FIBRES

Fibres reveal pith, *which is cut out*

First set of fibres

Section of bark
left between stripped fibres

3D VIEW

" BY UNPICKING THE
FIBRES YOU ARE
UNPICKING THE **NATURE**
OF WOOD ITSELF. "

FOCUS ON...

STRIPPING WOOD FIBRES

Wood fibres have a natural tendency to "run off"; *see* p18. Here, once you have worked around the stick pulling off short fibres, there are then enough layers so that even though the peeled fibres run off, the bonds between layers are strong enough to maintain them as a strip.

Initial fibres *run off the side*

First few *passes build layers that maintain further fibres as a strip*

Continuous strips *can be pulled once there is enough wood for the fibres to run into*

The Process

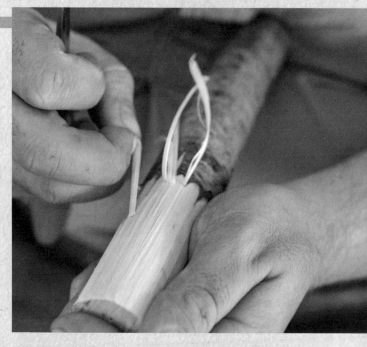

1 Start off the fibres

Using forehand grip, shave bark from a third of the rod, being careful to remove as little wood as possible. Pluck at fibres at the sawn end with the blade tip, and start pulling off slithers.

Knife grips: Forehand, thumb pull – see pp39, 21

Use thumb pull grip *to pluck fibres*

2 Pull to full length

The first slithers will quickly run off to the sides and tear out. Keep plucking with the knife and pulling with your fingers, moving around the circumference of the rod, until eventually you are able to pull fibres down the entire length. This may take several passes and must not be rushed, since we are relying on the natural running off of fibres to set the conditions for finally being able to draw the fibres in long strips.

Cut diagonally *through the pith, then pare it back*

Fold back over *the first set of fibres*

Thicker fibres *can be split in half again*

3 Cut off the pith

Continue going round and round the rod, plucking and pulling the fibres. Eventually there will be no more full-length fibres to pull, and you will hit the pith at the centre. At this point, simply cut off the pith with the knife in chest lever grip, or saw it off with a pull saw.

Knife grip: Chest lever – see p19

Technique: Using a pull saw – see p24

4 Strip the handle side

Shave bark off the other half, stopping 19mm (¾in) from the first fibres to leave a band of bark. Repeat steps 1–3, but stop pulling fibres when the rod reaches a diameter of around 19mm (¾in) to leave a handle. Cut a chamfer at the end of the handle using thumb pull grip.

Technique: Carving a chamfered edge – see p16

CONTINUED ☛

WEAVING THE BINDING

1. Take one end of the strip, form a loop big enough to squeeze on to the bristles but small enough to hold position, then tightly tie in the end.

2. Take the other end of the strip and weave it through and around the original loop, making several passes, if necessary, until you are happy with the thickness and strength of the loop.

Adjust the tension *on either side to run the split straight*

5 Baton the second rod

The binding ring is created from the same material as the brush, split over and over again until you have a thin ribbon. First baton the rod in half, starting the split with a knife and small mallet, and continuing with your hands. You need to control the split by putting tension into the side you wish the split to run into. A great way to do this is by bracing each side of the split with your thumbs.

Technique: Batoning with a knife – see p16

Fibre tension *stops the split running off to the side*

6 Split down to a pliable strip

Keep splitting the wood in half and half again. When splitting a thinner splint from a larger one, you can focus all of your efforts into stretching the thick side by using both arms to bend the stick across your knee. Keep splitting until you end up with a thin, fairly pliable strip of wood.

TIP
Wood cleft tangentially — where you are keeping layers of growth rings intact — makes the best binding.

Design variations

Once you've got the knack of stripping fibres you can experiment with different sizes of brush. Or try a more rough-and-ready way of delaminating wood to make a renewable alternative to a scouring pad.

Long-handled broom

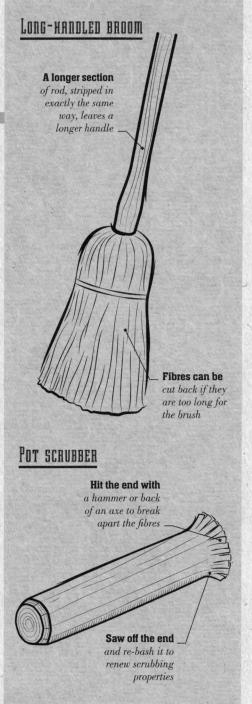

A longer section *of rod, stripped in exactly the same way, leaves a longer handle*

Fibres can be *cut back if they are too long for the brush*

Pot scrubber

Hit the end with *a hammer or back of an axe to break apart the fibres*

Saw off the end *and re-bash it to renew scrubbing properties*

Cut off *the ends using thumb pull grip*

7 Weave a binding ring

Work a shallow bend into the strip by bending it around your knee, then make tighter bends with your fingers, working along the strip, until it is flexible enough to be woven. Weave the strip into a ring that fits tightly over the top of the fibres; *see* Weaving the binding, above left. Gently pull the ends to tighten the ring, then cut off the excess.

CHAPTER 02

AXEWORK

All the projects in this chapter take as their starting point splitting a log and shaping with an axe. As you work through, you will develop increasing precision and tackle simple joinery.

MAKE A
MALLET

A large mallet is an essential bit of kit for hitting an axe, a froe, or wedges to split logs. Mallets take a fair beating in their lifetime, and will often wear through until the end is too weak; if this happens, simply saw off the end to leave a smaller mallet. Wooden mallets must be used on axes and metal wedges, rather than metal hammers, which are more likely to deform the wedge and can produce dangerous flying metal splinters.

YOU WILL NEED

TOOLS & EQUIPMENT
- Handsaw
- Axe block
- Axe
- Straight knife

MATERIALS
- 1 log of green wood, between 130–180mm (5–8in) in diameter and around 750mm (29½in) in length; a softer wood will be easier to carve, but a harder wood will make a more enduring mallet

SKILLS

YOU WILL LEARN TO
- Using a handsaw: *step 2*
- Shape with an axe: *steps 3–5*

REMIND YOURSELF HOW TO
- Carve a chamfered edge: *p16*

KNIFE GRIPS
- Thumb pull: *p21*
- Forehand: *p39*

DESIGN GUIDE

Try to select a log with a knotty section for the hitting end of the mallet. Size the handle according to what's comfortable for you to grip, though any less than 38mm (1½in) will make it too weak.

1. FACETED HANDLE

Start the taper *from about a third of the length*

Large knot *for hitting surface*

500mm (20in)

51mm (2in)

110mm (4 5/16in)

2. CHAMFERED END

Flare back out *towards the base*

Waste *wood*

Flat end *so that it stands up on its head*

SIDE VIEW

> **" THERE IS SIMPLY NO DECENT SHOP-BOUGHT ALTERNATIVE TO THIS KIND OF HANDMADE MALLET. "**

KNOTTY WOOD

Knots are grain configurations where there was once a branch growing out. They can be from a live branch or from a dead one absorbed into the trunk, called a "dead knot". Wood is weaker and most likely to split or delaminate on straight sections. Knotty grain is at an angle and interlocked with the straight grain, which prevents splitting from occuring so readily.

Interlocked grain *is harder and less likely to split when used as a hitting surface*

Side branch *forms a knot in the log*

The Process

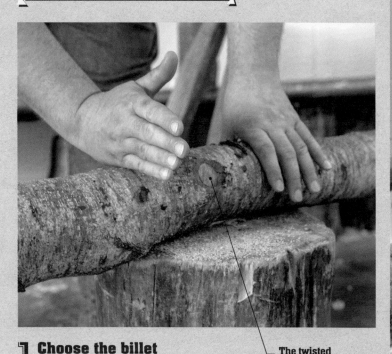

The twisted grain *of knotty wood makes it more resilient*

1 Choose the billet
Assess the log and identify the section of wood you want for the mallet. Ideally, it should be a section with a knot on one side to provide a harder impact area for the hitting face, but with knot-free wood above or below for the handle; *see* Knotty wood, above.

2 Saw the billet
Use a handsaw to cut out the billet. Place the log on an axe block, resting the knee of your supporting side on the log to steady it and using your thumb or index finger to guide the blade. Saw as close to the edge of the block as possible to prevent the wood from tipping, and saw downwards at around a 45° angle; if you tried to saw horizontally, the log would simply roll on the block.

1.

2.

1. Chopping cuts create chips by cutting across the fibres at an angle of around 30°, which the wedge of the axe then splits along the grain.

2. A more vertical action with gentler force can then be employed to remove the chips and make finer cuts. These shaving cuts use the bevel of the blade to guide the cutting edge, affording greater control.

3 Rough shape the handle

Begin to square and shape the handle, starting cuts from just below the knotty head. When taking thick shavings, it may help to lever open the previous cut before taking the next swing, giving you a wider target; or leave the ax in the cut and bump axe and mallet down on the block, to split wood off.

Start to taper *the handle towards the mallet base*

Make the facets *fairly neat and uniform*

4 Facet the handle

Take off the corners of your initial shaping and refine the handle by cutting a series of eight facets, so that it has a roughly octagonal shape viewed in cross-section. Make the facets broadly equal in width, with the edges running in parallel lines towards the end; if the handle tapers too much it can be hard to hold.

CONTINUED ☞

Keep your thumb

Keep your thumb *offset from the direction of the blade and tucked behind the handle*

Try to give *the surfaces as smooth a finish as possible*

5 Shave down to size

Once you've shaped your eight sides, keep shaving them down in turn to reduce the width of the handle until it's comfortable to grip but not so thin that it loses strength. As you reduce the girth, also shape the handle so that it flares out slightly towards the bottom, rather than tapering to a point.

6 Chamfer the end

Cut a chamfer at the handle's end; this prevents the wood from chipping and improves the comfort of the grip. The top of the mallet could also be chamfered, but make the chamfer much thinner so that the mallet can still be stored balanced on its head.

Technique: Carving a chamfered edge – see p16

Knife grip: Thumb pull – see p21

Knife grip: Forehand – see p39

Design variations

The split-log mallet is easier to make than it looks, provided you mark the sawing depth with tape and control the splits. The tapered-joint mallet draws on reaming skills used for the leg joints in the Raised Axe Block project; *see* p56.

SPLIT-LOG MALLET

Saw to the depth *of the handle, all round the log*

Split the wood *down from the handle end, in small sections, to remove waste*

TAPERED-JOINT MALLET

Flared end *fits securely in tapered hole*

Drilled hole *is reamed to a taper*

Metal bands *to help hold together the wood fibres*

7 Dress the handle
Finally, take off any untidy edges, sharp points, and rough patches from the handle. The forehand grip works well for this, as it allows you to take off long, thin shavings. Resting the mallet on an axe block, position the knife at a slight diagonal with the tip pointing upwards, and simply shave down the length of the handle, cutting with the part of the blade closest to the handle.

Cut off the *corners to give a 45° bevel*

MAKE A

RAISED AXE BLOCK

This is an essential bit of axework kit for the remaining projects in the book, and fitting the legs gives you a simple introduction to joinery, since tapered tenons are strong but forgiving of minor inaccuracies. When using, adopt a wide stance, with the leg on your dominant side a step back, so that it isn't in the way if you accidentally swing the axe through.

YOU WILL NEED

TOOLS AND EQUIPMENT

- Axe
- Mallet
- Wedges
- Pencil and compass
- Auger 25mm (1in) in diameter
- Protractor
- Sliding bevel
- Tape
- Straight knife

MATERIALS

- 1 log of green wood, around 150mm (5⅞in) in diameter and 760mm (30in) in length, for the legs

- 1 log of green or dry wood, around 305mm (12in) in diameter and 430mm (17in) deep, for the block; a softer wood is easier to carve, but if the block will be kept outside you may want a more durable wood and/or one with more tannin, to slow the rot

SKILLS

YOU WILL LEARN TO

- Split a log with an axe and wedges: *steps 1–3*
- Form a tapered tenon joint: *steps 5–12*
- Drill angled holes: *step 8*
- Ream with a knife: *step 9*

REMIND YOURSELF HOW TO

- Shape with an axe: *p50*
- Use an auger: *p30*

KNIFE GRIPS

- Thumb pull: *p21*
- Chest lever: *p19*
- Shin pull: *p63*

DESIGN GUIDE

The top of the block should be around waist height. There is enough mass in the block to cope with the impact from the axe without vibrating too much. The legs are wide apart for stability without being constant trip hazards, and can be removed for easy storage.

300mm (11¹³/₁₆in)

500mm (19¹¹/₁₆in)

Top of the block *sits at a comfortable working height*

Legs fitted *with tapered tenon and mortise joints*

Tailor to waist height

SIDE VIEW

TIP

When you start chasing the split, hold the axe to prevent it falling out, and to help keep the log stable.

> ❝ CAREFULLY AXE APART ANY FIBRES STILL ATTACHED, WATCHING WHERE THE SWING MAY FOLLOW THROUGH. ❞

The Process

1 Start the split

Take the longer log and rest it against the fat log that will form the block piece. Position the blade of the axe across the centre of a cut end and give the axe head a few solid taps with the mallet, until the blade is submerged and the wood is beginning to split down the fibres.

2 Chase the split

With the axe still embedded, rest the log horizontally and, gripping the handle of the axe, tap in the first wedge close to the limit of the split. Knock in a second wedge to continue the split. This will loosen the first wedge, which you can then knock in beyond the second wedge. Continue chasing the split until the log is cloven in two.

Hold the axe *straight upright and centred*

Start shaving *just beyond midpoint and flip to work the other half*

3 Split each half again

Rest one of the log halves flat side-down on the axe block and split it in half again. Employ the same method, but make the initial split with the axe at the midpoint of the log. As the wood gets thinner the risk of running off increases (*see* p18), and by splitting from the middle you are effectively halving this risk. Repeat with the other log half, and then pick the three best log pieces, most evenly matched in girth, for the legs. As an alternative to this technique you could use a cleaving brake and froe; *see* p130.

4 Dress the leg

Work over a leg piece with the axe, removing the outer and inner bark, which make the wood more prone to rotting, and smoothing the surface; keep your supporting hand well away from the chopping action. The raised axe block will be "flat-packable" and the legs will be handled frequently, so it is important to remove any splinters and sharp edges. Don't chop away too much wood, though, to maintain leg strength.

Technique: Shaping with an axe – see p50

CONTINUED ☛

TAPERED TENON JOINT

Since a tapered joint relies upon accuracy of the taper gradient rather than sizing, slight discrepancies don't affect fit, and when the tenon shrinks, it simply moves further into the mortise. It is also great for flat-packing, since it can be freed from a tight fit with a simple tap, whereas a straight tenon must be forced out along its whole length.

A tapered tenon *will always fit neatly*

A straight tenon *will no longer fit if it shrinks*

Position roughly *in the middle of the end face*

5 Mark the tenon width

Pick the straighter end of the dressed leg for the tapered tenon. Mark the minimum width with a circle 25mm (1in) in diameter, positioned roughly in the middle of the end face. A good way to do this is by screwing the auger in a short way to leave a dimple.

6 Cut the taper

Axe the tenon to shape, starting from about 75mm (2¹⁵⁄₁₆in) up the leg, until it has tapered down close to the correct diameter with a small amount of waste. Keep checking the end as you cut, to see if you are nearing the guideline. Alternatively, a draw knife and shaving horse are useful for shaping the tenon, since you can see the diameter guide as you shave; *see* p94. Repeat steps 4–6 to make the other legs.

Keep the auger aligned in two planes as you drill: straight forwards on the sightline and at angle of splay.

For a tripod like this the sightlines dissect the other two holes, so that the feet of the legs will match the same equilateral triangle, only bigger; here we have marked one sightline in chalk for clarity.

Line up the sliding bevel with the splay angle parallel with the sightline. Get someone else to sight, or check the bevel alignment after every few turns of the auger.

7 Mark the leg positions

Determine the position of the legs on the underside of the block. Work out the spacing by marking an equilateral triangle (all internal angles 60°) on the block face. The triangle should be centred, and of a size so that the legs are neither too close together, nor too near the edge of the block, and avoiding any splits in the log.

Mark out the leg positions with chalk

8 Start the mortise holes

Set the angle of splay for the legs. An angle of 30° from the vertical usually works well, but test by holding the legs in place to see if it looks good and is practical. Use a protractor to set the angle on a sliding bevel. Cut the initial holes for the legs by drilling in the auger at the angle of the bevel and to a depth of 75mm (2^{15}⁄$_{16}$in). It is vital to maintain correct alignment as you drill; *see* Cutting angled holes, above.

Mark the drilling depth with tape to act as a guide

CONTINUED ☞

REAMING THE HOLES

Reaming can be done with a specialist drill attachment called a reamer, which is the most accurate way of doing it. When reaming with a knife, it is easiest going into the end grain, and much more difficult if the grain runs horizontally through the hole. Always keep the tip of the knife in the hole so that it does not slip out.

1. **Take chamfers** *off the corners*

2.

3. **Continue** *chamfering until conical*

9 Ream the mortise holes

Use a knife to cut sloping sides to the mortise holes so that they mirror the conical tenons; called "reaming". Widen each hole to 35mm (1⅜in) in diameter and mark the additional width to remove. Cut a chamfer to this line, then cut deeper in by successively taking off the corners of this initial chamfer; *see* Reaming the holes, above. When making twisting cuts, it can help to use your other hand to support and act as a pivot point, for more control. Always keep the tip of the knife in the hole so there's no risk of it slipping out.

10 Shave tenons

Make final shaping cuts to the leg tenons so that they fit the mortises. Make sure you have enough wood for the widest point of the reamed hole; the depth of the hole lets you know where that thickness is needed on the tenon. First cut a chamfer at the end to the circle guideline, using thumb pull grip. Switch to chest lever grip to shave off the waste left from the initial shaping. If your supporting arm gets tired, use shin pull grip so you can rest the leg on your thigh; *see* above right.

Knife grips: Thumb pull, chest lever – see pp21, 19

Lock the knife into position between your shin and knee, with the back of the blade resting against your leg.

To effect the cut, hold the knife still and draw the wood back towards you.

Hold the edge of the blade at an angle and draw the wood diagonally across it.

Design variations

The basic block can be adapted to give upright surfaces for additional support in the chopping area. And fitting shorter legs to a halved log makes an easy, rough-and-ready bench.

BENCH

Leg joints *can be pegged for stability; see p130*

Fit blind tenons *to an outdoor bench, to stop rain getting into the joints*

BACKED BLOCK

Saw out *a segment of the block to create a back for supporting billets*

Cut a notch *for shaping objects like spoons, so that the handles can dangle securely*

PEGGED BLOCK

Wooden block *fitted as a back support*

Peg the block *by inserting dowling into drilled holes*

Scuff marks *on the tenon reveal where material must be removed*

11 Test the fit

As you shave the tenons, keep testing the fit by knocking the leg firmly into its mortise. Look for tell-tale scuff marks on the tenon, which indicate where the tenon is slightly too big and causing friction. Shave off these raised areas with the knife. Note that if you increase the angle of taper for a better fit, you may need to start the taper further back on the leg to maintain a straight line. If you struggle to get the legs out, tap them on the sides with the mallet: the vibrations have a loosening effect.

MAKE A
COAT PEG

Over millions of years, trees have evolved the shape and grain orientation of side branches to build in great strength at the join. It's difficult to think of another green wood artefact that takes a lighter touch with what nature already has to offer.

YOU WILL NEED

TOOLS & EQUIPMENT
- Axe block
- Axe
- Handsaw (such as a pull saw)
- Drill and 3mm (⅛in) drill bit
- Straight knife
- *optional:* Plywood offcut

MATERIALS
- A forked branch section, around 230mm (9¹⁄₁₆in) long and 25mm (1in) diameter; it is usually best when the secondary branch has a slightly narrower diameter
- 40mm (1⁹⁄₁₆in) screws

SKILLS

YOU WILL LEARN TO
- Make a square countersink: *steps 6–7*

REMIND YOURSELF HOW TO
- Use an electric drill: *p24*
- Carve a chamfered edge: *p16*

KNIFE GRIPS
- Chest lever: *p19*
- Thumb pull: *p21*
- Thumb pivot: *p22*

DESIGN GUIDE

The main considerations of the design involve the practicalities of fixing the peg: a flat back; screw points that don't spoil the appearance; and a hook length that allows access for a screwdriver.

Chamfered finish *to all three ends*

An offset branch *makes the perfect natural hook*

Flat side *for fixing to wall or other surface*

SIDE VIEW

Branch sawn *to give clearance for screw holes*

Square countersinks *housing round screw holes*

FRONT VIEW

66 THIS SIMPLE PROJECT

MAKES USE OF THE

NATURAL SHAPE

OF BRANCHES. 99

> " FOR A STRONG PEG YOU WANT A NICE WIDE SURFACE AGAINST THE WALL. "

TIP
The secondary branch is less prone to splitting, as it is held together by the primary branch.

The Process

1 Flatten the back
Rest the wood on the block and use an axe to chop and shave a flat surface to the side opposite the offset branch. Chop until you get just beyond the pith; when left in the round, wood tends to split, so by removing slightly more than half of the wood you are creating a stronger, semi-cylindrical shape.

Chop to the middle *then flip it round to shave the other half*

2 Trim the side branch
The length of the hook should be long enough to be functional, but not so long that you do not have room to insert the top screw. Saw off as much of the side branch as is needed to give clearance for a screwdriver, using a pull saw or other type of handsaw. Hold the blade raised up at an angle to avoid catching the main branch, but cut straight across.

Technique: Using a pull saw – see p24

Guide the blade *with the thumb or finger of your supporting hand*

3 Drill screw holes

Position the drill at the centre point of your piece of wood, about 25mm (1in) from the top, and drill straight down all the way through. If you find the drill is running off target, you can usually correct this by angling the drill for the first couple of seconds so the drill bit can fit comfortably in the groove you have made, then adjusting your angle so you are drilling straight downwards. Drill another hole in the same position at the opposite end of the coat peg.

Technique: Using an electric drill – see p24

4 Shave the back

Refine the rough axed surface of the back of the peg with a knife in chest lever grip, making it as flat and smooth as you can. Complete one half first, before flipping the peg round to work down the other half. You are essentially repeating the actions you took in step 1 with the axe, but to a more refined finish.

Knife grip: Chest lever – see p19

Check that the wood *is flat by holding it against the wall or another flat surface*

CONTINUED ☞

Use your arm *as a pivot to guide the knife*

5 Chamfer the ends

Use the thumb pull grip to cut chamfers around the three end points of the peg, and shave off any sawn surfaces, to give your coat peg a neater finish. At this point, if you prefer a less rustic look, you could remove all of the bark or even carve the surface to create a more refined design.

Don't chamfer the edges *that need to sit flush against the wall*

Technique: Carving a chamfered edge – see p16

Knife grip: Thumb pull – see p21

6 Start the countersink

Rest your cutting arm on the axe block so it doesn't slip. Hold the peg flat on the block with one hand, and hold the knife in the other; your knife hand should be in a fist with the blade directed away from you. Without removing any wood, make four incisions, each about 2mm (1/16in) or so in length, at the corner points of the hole.

> " CARVING A SQUARE COUNTERSINK AROUND THE SCREW HOLES NOT ONLY LOOKS GOOD, IT IS ALSO EASIER THAN CARVING A ROUND COUNTERSINK. "

7 Cut the countersink

Using the thumb pivot grip, cut out the sections between the points of the cross to form a square. Resting your hand on the block gives you more control, so you don't slip with the tip of the knife. Rest the end of the peg on the block and pivot it as you cut. Cut diagonally down into the hole with the tip of the knife, then remove each section of the countersink bit by bit. Repeat steps 6–7 on the other hole.

Knife grip: Thumb pivot – see p22

8 Let the peg dry

If using very green wood, screw your coat peg on to a scrap of plywood to keep it straight while it dries. This method is also useful if you are making several pegs and don't intend to put them up right away. It is also advisable to spread some PVA glue on the exposed end grain of the secondary branch, to protect it against splitting.

Design variations

Depending on the size and shape of your branch, you can create a range of handy objects for use in your hallway or around your home using branches like this one. For instance, two of these coat pegs could be used to hold up a curtain rail.

MULTI-HOOK

Several secondary *branches on the same side can offer multiple hooks*

COAT STAND

Whole branch *with side branches on opposite sides*

Branch fitted *to log half with a tenon joint; see Shrink Pot p108*

MAKE A
COOKING SPOON

A spoon is one of the first tools we ever use as babies, and the simple appearance belies a surprisingly complex design that takes practice to get right. With this project you will get to grips with carving a hollow in the bowl of a spoon and shaping the convex back of the bowl into the neck.

YOU WILL NEED

EQUIPMENT
- Axe, axe block, and mallet
- Straight knife
- Spoon knife

MATERIALS
- 1 log of green wood, around 125mm (4¹⁵⁄₁₆in) in diameter and 200mm (7⅞in) in length

SKILLS

YOU WILL LEARN TO
- Carve a bowl shape: *steps 2–3, 8, 13–15*
- Use a bent knife: *steps 16–19*

REMIND YOURSELF HOW TO
- Split with an axe: *p56*
- Shape with an axe: *p50*
- Carve a chamfered edge: *p16*

KNIFE GRIPS
- Reinforced pull: *p32*
- Thumb pivot: *p22*
- Chest lever: *p19*
- Thumb pull: *p21*
- Thumb push: *p22*
- Shin pull: *p63*

DESIGN GUIDE

The relatively thick, blunt rim of the bowl is designed to protect the spoon from the daily wear and tear of cooking. A wide handle with a rounded end is comfortable for gripping as you vigorously stir food around a pan. The hollow is fairly shallow, as this spoon is intended for stirring rather than scooping up. For the order and direction of cuts, refer to the diagrams on pp77 and 80.

Top of the spoon *is carved on the bark side*

Spoon blank *is split out tangentially*

LOG CROSS SECTION

Handle facets *finish with a chamfered end for comfort*

Pinched neck *narrows to two facets, forming a ridge*

200mm (7⅞in)

25mm (1in)

65mm (2½in)

Peaked edge *for scraping the bottom of pots*

OVERHEAD VIEW

66 A SPOON CARVED BY HAND IS A TRADITIONAL TOKEN OF LOVE
BECAUSE OF THE SKILL NEEDED TO CARVE A REALLY GOOD ONE. **99**

> 66 OUT OF THE BLANK, WITH JUST A FEW CHOPS AND SHAVES OF THE AXE, THE RUDIMENTARY SHAPE OF A SPOON QUICKLY BEGINS TO FORM. 99

The Process

1 Split out a blank

Split out a quarter log and shave to around 5mm (³⁄₁₆in) wider than the finished spoon; if very wide, chop or cleave further to quickly reduce the size. Take the peak off the back, removing at least the pith and the first couple of growth rings.

Techniques: Splitting with an axe, shaping with an axe – see pp56, 50

The bark *side will form the top of the spoon*

Cut long *shavings from the middle*

2 Facet the back

Working on the non-bark side of the blank, begin to shape the back of the bowl of the spoon by chopping two facets down the corner edges of each side. You want to end up with three equal-sized facets across the back, and two square edges on the sides. For safety, and to control your cuts, always chop from the middle, flipping the blank around to chop the other way.

Make angled *chops to split the fibres*

3 Start to shape handle

Chop out some of the side bulk, taking waste from just below the start of the bowl. When carving into the neck at the top of the handle, be very careful not to cut your spoon supporting hand. You shouldn't be swinging with your arm at this stage, instead use very controlled flicks of the axe, making sure not to lift the axe high enough that it could come down on to your supporting hand.

4 Round the bowl forwards

Round the bowl on a second plane by chopping two facets forwards, from just beyond the middle of the bowl to the front edge. Create these curves by executing "bump cuts": place the axe where you want to make the cut; tilt it until you feel the edge bite into the wood; then lift together both axe and blank, and "bump" them down onto the block to effect the cut. Change the angle slightly with each bump cut to create a rough dome shape.

"Bump cut" *right to the front edge of what will be the bowl*

CONTINUED ☞

TIP

If you don't create a break in the fibres before shaping the crank, there's a risk you will split off the entire top of the bowl.

Keep the cuts *close together and chop out the waste*

Take off the corners *either side of the central cut*

5 Relieve the crank

The next stage is to shape the crank of the spoon, which is the slope between the handle and the bowl. Before shaping, however, you need to you need to break up the fibres where the lowest point of the crank will be, by making a series of shallow chops straight across the centre of the bowl.

6 Angle the crank

Starting on the handle side, chop diagonally down from where you want to begin the neck into the first part of the bowl. The tip of the axe does most of the work and shouldn't go beyond the initial vertical cuts made in the previous step.

7 Start the hollow

Turn the blank around and make similar sloping cuts from the bowl side, back towards the centre of the bowl.

Chop on the edge *of the block to stop the axe*

8 Rough shape the handle

Chop out most of the waste from the back of the handle, still following the facets set in step 2. Remove the outer and inner bark from the top side. Then remove most of the bulk from the back of the handle; in particular, remove waste at the back shoulders, and take cuts into the neck.

Side facets *should curve in at the neck*

CONTINUED ☞

> ❝ AS YOU FACET THE RIM, FEEL FOR WHEN THE GRAIN CHANGES DIRECTION, THEN FLIP THE SPOON AND PUSH THE BLADE THE OTHER WAY. ❞

10 Refine the neck

Return to reinforced pull strokes to further shape the neck. Neaten up the axe cuts and create a narrower shape to the neck by taking cuts in tighter from both sides, as well as from the top and bottom.

Start cuts *at the bowl and continue down the handle*

9 Dress the bowl

Switching to knifework, refine the top surface of the bowl with reinforced pull grip, working your way from the rim back towards the neck; notice the thumb tucked safely behind the spoon. You should be able to take shavings all the way into the neck by angling the blade, but you may need to come back down the handle towards the bowl, using thumb pivot grip.

Knife grips: Reinforced pull, thumb pivot – see pp32, 22

CUTS TO THE BACK

This diagram offers a guide to the direction of shaping cuts required at the back of the spoon, and the best grips to effect them. The trickiest part to carve is the shoulder of the bowl and into the neck, where you are shaping on several planes to form the sweeping convex and ridge.

a CHEST LEVER
b THUMB PUSH
c REINFORCED PULL

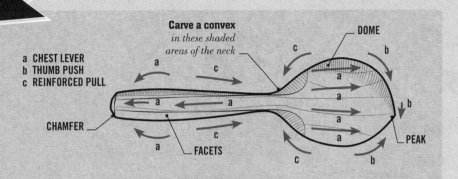

Carve a convex *in these shaded areas of the neck*

DOME

CHAMFER

FACETS

PEAK

You can use your supporting hand's thumb to steady the initial cut

11 Dome the bowl

Switch to chest lever grip to cut a dome shape to the back of the bowl of the spoon. Refine the convex shape begun with the axework by cutting multiple short facets. Cut in the direction of the bowl rim, remembering to bring the top of the rim to an asymmetrical peak.

Knife grip: Chest lever – see p19

12 Neaten the back

Cut a square facet around the rim of the bowl using thumb push grip. Blend a convex curve into the neck with reinforced pull. Then refine the handle facets with chest lever, switching to shin pull grip if you start to get tired.

Knife grips: Thumb push, shin pull – see pp22, 63

Smooth the surface *by taking long, thin shavings*

CONTINUED ☞

TIP

When cutting the neck, you can press the fingers of your reinforcing hand on the back of the blade to help direct it.

13 Pinch in the neck

Remove more material from the neck, making cuts with reinforced pull. Take shavings from all sides, but try not to lose too much depth: you are aiming to pinch in the neck to a keel-like narrow ridge where it joins the bowl, which gradually widens out to three broad facets down the length of the handle.

Start the **ridge** *from the shoulder of the dome*

14 Shape and chamfer the handle

Finish shaping the handle with chest lever grip, flaring it out before tapering it back in slightly towards the end. Dress the handle with long thin shavings for a smooth finish. Cut a chamfer into the end of the handle using thumb pull grip; chamfering gives a neat finish, prevents fibres furring, and makes the spoon comfortable to hold.

Technique: Carving a chamfered edge – see p16

Knife grip: Thumb pull – see p21

When carving a curve, there is a midpoint beyond which, if you keep cutting, the blade will catch on the ends of the fibres and tear into the wood. This is why we say to carve down hill to the bottom of the valley.

Fibres compress *in the direction of the grain*

Exposed fibre ends *catch on the blade edge beyond the centre line*

15 Finish the edges
Returning to reinforced pull, cut the corners off all edges to remove any sharp points and refine the finish. Cut a wide facet into the edge at the front of the bowl, along the side that culminates in the offset peak, which will form the scraping area of the spoon. Use thumb push to cut this facet.

Continuous *shavings give a smooth finish*

16 Hollow the bowl
Draw a pencil guideline to set the extent of the hollow, leaving a fairly wide rim. Use a spoon knife for hollowing out; *see* p81. Take small shavings initially, and start on the far side of the bowl, which is more difficult to cut as the guiding bevel of the blade has less wood to rest on. Use the thumb pull grip as shown above, with your thumb safe behind the spoon and supported on your leg so it doesn't slip. Cut directly across the grain and build up the length of shavings to reach the far side of the spoon.

Manually guide *the edge of the blade into the cut, on the far side*

CONTINUED ☞

FOCUS ON...
CUTS TO THE TOP

Hollowing out the bowl is the main challenge when carving the top, requiring several changes of grip. When shaping the curves, aim to think in quadrants to avoid digging into the grain; *see* Cutting to the centre, p79.

a **THUMB PULL**
b **REINFORCED PULL**
c **THUMB PUSH** with edge reversed
d **THUMB PUSH**
e **CHEST LEVER**

FACETS   RIDGE   THICK RIM   HOLLOW

Follow the **curve** *but don't cross the centre line*

17 Shave to depth and smooth off

Check the thickness of the bowl walls using your finger and thumb as a guide: you are aiming for less than 6mm (⅜in), more than 3mm (⅛in). Always cut towards the middle of the hollow, and stop when you reach an imaginary centre line; *see* Cutting to the centre, p79. Build up to longer shavings, which will take the bowl deeper. Once you've reached the right depth, smooth the surface with sweeping shaves.

18 Employ the reversed thumb push

Chasing a shaving around the quadrant's rim can be tricky with other grips. Come at it instead with a variation of thumb pivot grip, whereby the blade is reversed from its usual position and you push the blade edge across the grain.

A spoon knife has a convex curving blade, which allows it to cut smoothly on the concave surface of a hollow.

Effect cuts using the same grips as for a straight knife, and following the same safety tips, such as here keeping the thumb tucked behind in thumb pull grip.

19 Smooth out the grooves

Hollowing out the bowl leaves small grooves on the rim. Smooth these off by cutting wide shavings around the inner edge. You will need to use different grips to get at all four quadrants of the rim: thumb pull, reinforced pull, and thumb push with the edge of the blade reversed.

Remove the *corners of the rim and the pencil lines*

Design variations

The shape of the bowl is a good place to start experimenting. An oval or circular shape with a thin rim is right for an eating spoon, while tapering tips and squarer sides are good for scraping, stirring, and serving.

FIG SPOON

Rounded "fig" shape *and shallow bowl make for comfortable eating*

Thin handle *gets strength from flexibility*

EGG SPOON

Egg shape *is good for stirring tea or, indeed, digging into a boiled egg*

Experiment *with decorative flourishes to the handle outline*

SHOVEL SPOON

Rectilinear *bowl is useful for flipping food and serving*

Fat handle *designed to be gripped in the flat of the palm*

MAKE A
BOWL

This elegant bowl incorporates handles and a relatively shallow and elongated hollow, making it perfect for serving food. You will learn to work with an adze and bowl gouge, and gain insights into coping with the changing direction of grain when chopping out and carving a hollow form.

YOU WILL NEED

TOOLS & EQUIPMENT

- Mallet and froe
- Axe and axe block
- Pencil and measuring equipment
- Workbench with upright supports and wedges
- Adze or gouge with metal end to handle and small mallet
- Bowl gouge
- Hook knife, scorp, or dogleg gouge
- Push knife
- Handsaw (such as a pull saw)
- Straight knife
- *optional:* Draw knife, holdfast

MATERIALS

- A green wood log, around 250mm (9¹³⁄₁₆in) in diameter and 360mm (14³⁄₁₆in) in length

SKILLS

YOU WILL LEARN TO

- Split with a froe: *steps 1–3*
- Use an adze: *steps 8–9, 11*
- Measure thickness: *step 10*
- Use a bowl gouge: *step 12*
- Use a push knife: *step 17*

REMIND YOURSELF HOW TO

- Shape with an axe: *p50*
- Use a draw knife: *p94*
- Use a hook knife: *p70*
- Use a pull saw: *p24*

KNIFE GRIPS

- Spoon knife: *p74*
- Thumb push: *p22*
- Thumb pull: *p21*

DESIGN GUIDE

The diameter of the log largely determines the type of bowl that can be carved. The size we used is big enough for a large eating bowl. A wider log would be needed for a salad or fruit bowl, and narrower log for a small eating bowl or cup.

Hollow of the bowl *is carved from the rounded bark side*

Billet avoids *the pith and first few annular rings*

BILLET

Rim expands *to form handles at the narrower ends of the hollow*

Rim dips *and rises along the sides of the hollow*

Aim for *a thickness of 10mm (⅜in) to the non-handle areas of the bowl*

Slightly convex *shape to the sweep up to the handles*

SIDE VIEW

"HANDLES LEND VERSATILITY, AS WELL AS ADDING STRENGTH TO THE SHORT END GRAIN."

> ❝ IT IS IMPORTANT TO ACHIEVE A **SMOOTH FLAT SURFACE** TO THE BASE SIDE, FOR **JUDGING THE DEPTH** OF THE BOWL. ❞

Some fibres *may remain attached and can be severed with an axe*

The Process

1 Start the first split

To form the billet, place the log on an axe block and line up the blade of the froe across the centre of the log. For the first hit, keep the arm holding the froe relaxed to avoid moving the blade as you hit it, and tap gently with the mallet. Once the blade has made the initial cut, give it a few more forceful knocks until it is fully submerged.

2 Chase the split

Now use the handle as a lever, pulling and pushing to chase the split down right through. Choose a half and draw guidelines for your billet, indicating where to make splits. Take the wood from above the pith and first few rings, and form a billet with three straight sides and a curved top, centred on the apex; ours was around 200mm (7⅞in) wide and 115mm (4½in) deep. Split away the sides; the splits may run off as they are near the edge, but you can correct this with an axe.

Your body *provides opposing force for the levering action with the froe*

Keep the fingers *of your supporting hand well away from the chopping action*

3 Split out the billet

Next split off the first couple of growth rings and pith. Still resting the log on the axe block, position the froe on the guideline, knock it in, then move to the floor to kneel on the log as you lever the split.

The blade *should be submerged in the wood*

4 True the sides

Refine the split surfaces with the axe. You are making them straight and smooth so that the billet will clamp to the workbench and you can be confident of the dimensions of the bowl. Resting the billet on the axe block, chop and shave with the axe to true the sides so that they are parallel. For a neater finish, keep the axe head more vertical and make skewed cuts.

Technique: Shaping with an axe – see p50

CONTINUED ☞

Take progressively *less material off each facet as you approach the final line of your curve*

5 Assess and true the curve

Roughly remove the outer bark to assess the curve of the billet. You are checking for trueness: is it wonky, raised on one side? Work facets around the curved surface, aiming to make the curve more shallow by taking most material from the middle facet. Once hollowed, this shape creates a new sweeping curve along the bowl as seen from the side.

6 Shave with a draw knife

If you have one, a draw knife will achieve a more consistent line to the top curve and a near final smooth finish. A draw knife allows greater control because you make cuts towards your body and can use the resistance of your body to control the blade. By contrast, with an axe you are pushing the blade away from your body and resistance is coming from the billet.

Technique: Using a draw knife – see p94

Hold diagonally, *lean in with elbows locked, and pull with your whole body, leading from your strong arm*

Employ a swinging action with the adze to chop out wood, keeping your body out of the line of the swing. Support your wrist with your other hand for greater control.

Strike the wood at an angle of around 30° to remove thick chips; too perpendicular and the blade won't penetrate, too shallow and it will only skim the surface.

To take more accurate shavings, turn the blade edge more to the horizontal, so the outside bevel rubs the wood, guiding the cut, and employ gentler strokes.

7 Draw the hollow

Curved surface facing up, mark the centre point of the billet, then lines dividing it into quadrants. The longer line should ideally be straight and central, but needs to follow the direction of the grain; this shouldn't be a problem if you have trued the sides correctly. Draw the shape of the hollow of the bowl, keeping the centre point in the middle.

Wedging *the billet between uprights is one way to secure it*

8 Start chopping out the hollow

Chop out an initial dimple from the centre of the hollow, using a curved adze (*see* above). This first dimple gives clearance for chips which would otherwise have nowhere to split off into. Chop out from this starting point, removing about 25mm (1in) of material at a time, steadily expanding downwards and out towards the rim line but stopping slightly short.

CONTINUED ☞

FOCUS ON...

CUTTING OUT A HOLLOW

A hollow form must be excavated bit by bit, always working from the rim to the centre but not beyond. Most chips will come from the centre of the bowl, but accurately cutting into the end grain is the hard work. For the first cut onto the rim, it is best to aim for the inside of the rim and then adjust until your cuts are hitting accurately.

Most cuts *can be made radially towards the centre*

Use large, *confident chops for relatively smooth facets*

9 Expand the hollow

Once you have hollowed out to the initial depth, return to the centre and go deeper. Always chop towards the centre of the billet, going with the grain. If need be, stop chopping and remove loose chips so you can see what you're doing. A good practice is to chop out quadrant by quadrant, but it is not necessary to follow such a sequence. Continue chopping out the hollow until you think you are approaching a suitable depth.

10 Check base thickness

Measure the depth of the hollow to check the thickness of the base; a good thickness to aim for is 10–12mm (⅜–½in). You can try measuring with your finger and thumb, which are surprisingly accurate gauges of depth. For greater accuracy, take two rulers – or a ruler and anything else flat and straight – rest one on the rim and measure down with the other, then transfer this measurement to the side of the bowl.

Adopt a wide stance as if lunging forwards, with the leg on your weaker side foremost.

Grip with the handle end pressed into your palm, line up your forearm with the blade, and tuck in your elbow.

Push gently by bracing the gouge against your body and using your bodyweight for force.

Guide the blade with your weaker arm, ensuring the bevel is in contact with the wood to direct the edge. Keep your steadying arm resting on the billet or bench.

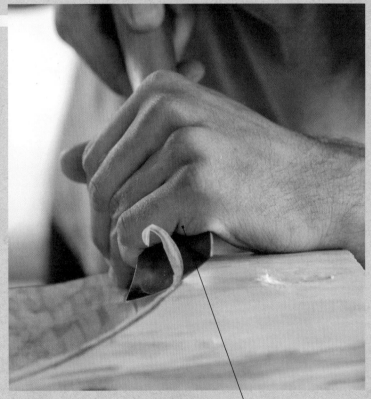

11 Start refining the surface

Employ "shaving mode" with the adze to cut an accurate line around the top edge, almost up to the line of the bowl rim. The blade edge of the adze should be closer to the horizontal for shallower cuts that take off less wood in thinner chips. Remember you are still cutting only as far as the centre and then changing direction. Once you have a neat edge around the rim, you can use more forceful cuts to even out the rest of the hollow. Do not get carried away trying to create a perfect finish at this point, though – you will do that with a gouge.

12 Refine with the gouge

Switch to using a bowl gouge to create a smoother finish (*see above*). Take off the corner of the rim with a thin chamfer. Work carefully: the more you can create the rim shape with a single cut to each quadrant, the neater the finish. Then dress the surface of the rest of the hollow, making refinements to the shape and aiming to get rid of marks left by the adze for a smooth finish; you can peel off wider shavings at this stage.

Don't be nervous *gripping fairly close to the blade edge: the direction of cut is away from your hand*

TIP
Keep the handle of the bowl knife as low as possible to engage the shallower section of the curved blade.

> ❝ TO MAKE ACCURATE SHAPING CUTS WITH AN AXE, MOVE YOUR HAND NEARER TO THE AXE HEAD AND SWITCH TO SHORTER SWINGS AND WRIST FLICKS. ❞

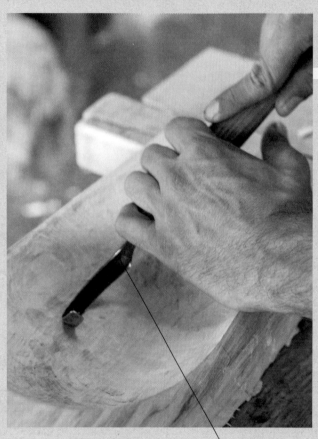

— **Rotate the blade** *rather than pulling it towards you*

13 Refine the centre of the hollow

You may struggle to reach all parts of the bowl with just one gouge. If you have problems getting into the curve at certain points in your bowl, switch to a tool with a tighter curve in the blade. For areas that regular, "stubbier" gouges cannot access – such as the tight space at the bottom of the hollow – you can use either a spoon knife, a scorp, or a dogleg gouge to smooth the surface.

Knife grip: Spoon knife – see p74

14 Draw the rim and dress the foot

Mark a guideline for the rim of the bowl, with a width of around 12mm (½in) at the thinnest point. Draw this outline parallel to the rim of the hollow, tapering it off to form the handles. Turn and reclamp the billet base-up. Use the bowl gouge to carve a level surface and smooth finish to what will become the foot of the bowl. Gouge straight across the grain at a 90° angle. It is best to dress the surface of the foot at this stage, before shaping, when the bowl can still be easily clamped; it also helps with shaping by marking out the foot.

15 Shape the body

Remove waste with an axe, chopping in relief cuts then shaving down. Again, only work up to the midpoint, taking off the corners of one side then turning the bowl around to remove the opposite corners. Follow the shape of the hollow and keep feeling for thickness, taking care at the thinnest points around the central band – at this point the grain changes direction, so a misplaced axe swing could be disastrous. Hold the axe nearer the head when more accurate cuts are needed, and switch to a knife for sections that follow the grain.

A good process *for the shaping is to work five facets down the length of the bowl*

16 Shape the handles and refine

Once you're happy with the rounded sides, work the sweep up to the handle; it can be attractive to give each sweep a slightly concave profile. Leave some waste beyond the handle ends, as protection against the impact these surfaces receive from the axing and shaving, and so you needn't worry about cutting the handles too short. Work over the whole surface again, removing large chop marks and ensuring a consistent shape and even thickness.

USING A PUSH KNIFE

Brace the piece to be worked with your body, securing it against an upright support on a workbench, or fix it in place with a block of waste wood and a holdfast, if you have one.

Close your fists around both of the knife's handles to grip, and make cuts by pushing with the blade held on the diagonal.

A push knife has a short bevel to allow for concave cuts; when working convex surfaces you need to avoid scooping in.

17 Shave a smooth finish

Finish the outside of the bowl with a push knife (*see* above), but leave a thin section around the rim untouched. Aim to cut a series of flat facets on the convex surfaces. As you move on to the sweep up to the handles, you can take more concave scoops; try to roll through in one motion to cut longer shavings. Alternatively, a draw knife, if you have one, makes quicker work of achieving a smooth finish.

18 Neaten the rim

Saw off most of the waste at the ends of the handles. Then use a knife and employ pull stroke to cut final crisp edges to the rim. If pull stroke becomes awkward as you move down the handles, switch to thumb pull grip. Dress the top surface to remove any rough patches and finger marks, using thumb push grip.

To avoid cutting *sections of rim base-side up, switch to thumb push grip*

Technique: Using a pull saw – see p24

Knife grips: Thumb pull, thumb push – see pp21, 22

Hold the bowl steady
and keep the thumb of your cutting hand safely tucked behind the bowl

19 Finish the handles

Chamfer each edge with thumb pull. Switch to thumb push to cut the handle curves, first chipping off pieces until you can blend the facets to a curve, then building up the curved end through a series of cuts from different angles. Return to pull stroke to peel off the sharp edge of the outer rim. Aim to remove the tiniest slither in a continuous shave. Do the same for the rim of the hollow, using either thumb pull or thumb push for different quadrants.

Design variations

Adding animal features is an ancient practice, and the sweeping form of a handle bowl suggests the shape of a bird. Bowls with steep, circular hollows have weaker structures, and these are best carved from wood with strong, interlocking grain: at a crook, from near the base of the tree, or from a burr.

BIRD BOWL

Minor shaping
adjustments can make a fantail

Taking wood
from the crook of a side branch can help form a raised head and tail

ROUND BOWL

Compact sides
are weaker due to short fibres, especially at the end grain

CUP BOWL

Drilled hole
for hanging

Single handle
instantly turns a small bowl into a cup

MAKE A
SERVING PLATTER

This simple platter is the perfect size for serving cheeses, presenting small cakes, or even using as an unconventional plate, and can double as a small chopping board. The project offers a good introduction to using a draw knife on a shaving horse, as well as practice at creating flat surfaces from cleft wood.

YOU WILL NEED

TOOLS & EQUIPMENT
- Mallet
- Froe
- Axe block
- Axe
- Pencil
- Shaving horse
- Draw knife
- Ruler
- Straight knife
- *optional*: Winding sticks

MATERIALS
- 1 green wood log, around 480mm (18⅞in) in length and 250mm (9¹³⁄₁₆in) in diameter

SKILLS

YOU WILL LEARN TO
- Correct wind: *steps 2–5*
- True with an axe: *step 3*
- Use a draw knife: *steps 7–10*

REMIND YOURSELF HOW TO
- Split with a froe: *p82*
- Carve a chamfered edge: *p16*

KNIFE GRIPS
- Thumb pivot: *p22*
- Thumb pull: *p21*
- Chest lever: *p19*
- Reinforced pull: *p32*

DESIGN GUIDE

The slim shape to the platter gives it elegance, and is also practical, leaving it light enough to carry in one hand. The long, wide paddle also helps with gripping and balance.

Handle starts *about a third of the way down*

4. ROUND CORNERS

470mm (18½in)

3. CURVE HANDLES

Edges of handle *are thickly chamfered*

115mm (4½in)

Bottom corners *are rounded off*

19mm (¾in)

OVERHEAD VIEW

2. SHAVE SIDES

1. SHAVE FACES

" WOOD TAKEN FROM THE RADIUS OF A LOG DOESN'T HAVE CURVED GROWTH RINGS WITHIN IT, AND SO THE PLATTER DRIES WITH MINIMAL CUPPING. "

CORRECTING WIND

Wood often splits with some kind of twist – or "wind" – in the grain. Winding sticks are simple tools to help you adjust for wind.

1. Place two straight sticks at either end of the billet and look across their top edges. The degree and points of misalignment indicate where to remove material to correct for wind.

2. Keep re-positioning the sticks as you true the billet: once they align everywhere along the plank, the wind has been removed.

The Process

1 Split and square

Split out a quarter log. Halve the quarter, cutting in line with one of the straight sides, then split in half again for two thin billets. Use the one that lay along the radius, known as "quartersawn": when the growth rings are short and vertical through the plank, rather than long and curved and horizontal, you are less likely to get cupping in the cross section of the plank. With an axe, start to make the sides of the billet squarer.

Technique: Splitting with a froe – see p82

2 Rough shape the board

Draw on the shape of the handle at the more twisted end, if there is one. Holding the other end of the billet, take out the waste around the outline of the handle, while at the same time correcting for wind; *see* above. Much of the wind can be removed when shaping the handle. Keep sighting down your billet to identify thick areas that need shaving down. Shape one side of the handle first, then get the other side to match.

Mark on crosses *where there are thicker areas to chop down*

A draw knife is an effective tool for cutting along fibres and quickly taking off shavings for a smooth finish that's hard to achieve with an axe and straight knife.

Cuts are effected by pulling with your whole body, holding the knife in both hands. This makes it much more powerful than a straight knife, allowing you to work much faster.

You can only use a draw knife by pulling it towards you; if the grain dips down and the knife follows the grain, making it difficult to take a straight cut, it may be best to turn the billet around and work that part in the other direction.

4 Shape the handle and flatten the edges

Turn the board on its side to shape one of the curved sides of the handle and smooth down the edge, then turn it over and shape the other side in the same way. Start by slicing off the corners, then round them off by removing any sharp points, checking all the time to ensure the shape is even.

3 Flatten the faces

Now use a draw knife to shave the surfaces of the platter flat and smooth; *see* above. Hold the knife on the diagonal, lock your elbows, and draw the blade towards you, pulling with your whole body. Shave one side of the board flat to create a datum surface, from which you can then flatten the other side by marking a parallel line along each edge.

Start the parallel
line from the point of minimum width

CONTINUED ☞

TIP
Rounding the end prevents "spelching": the splintering of fibres that occurs when wood is cut off across the grain.

5 Chamfer sides

Use pull stroke, but without reinforcement, to cut a thin chamfer on each of the long edges. You must use a "stop" to avoid cutting yourself: draw your elbow back close to your body and, with the tip of the knife slightly away from you, use a "cocked" wrist so that the inside of your wrist hits your chest first. Even out surface rough patches, using thumb pivot to get into nooks and crannies.

Technique: Carving a chamfered edge – see p16

Knife grip: Thumb pivot – see p22

Take care
around the unpredictable grain of knots

6 Round the ends

Shave the sawn surface smooth at the square end of the platter. First cut a wide chamfer along the edges with thumb pull grip, then switch to chest lever grip to cut between the chamfers; you may also find the reinforced pull grip useful for this step. Round off the corners by first cutting a bevel on the end, again with thumb pull grip.

Knife grips: Thumb pull, chest lever, reinforced pull – see pp21, 19, 32

> **" CURVED** PROFILES ARE SHAPED **PROGRESSIVELY** BY KNOCKING OFF A SERIES OF **CORNERS** AND BLENDING IN THE **EDGES. "**

**p your thumb
nd the handle,
of harm's way**

7 Refine the handle

Cut a wide chamfer on the handle, continuing the three facets you cut into the square edges. Switch between thumb pull and thumb pivot, depending on the direction you need to cut. When shaping curves, for concaves remember to cut each "side of the valley" separately, stopping at the valley base to avoid cutting against the grain. Push the board against your axe block to support it as you work.

Design variations

Drilling a hole into the handle allows a platter to be stored hanging up, but don't position it too close to the edge, to avoid weakness. Cutting a pair of asymmetrical platters is an economical use of a wider billet.

TWO-HANDLED PLATTER

Handles at both ends *enable a longer board to be carried*

Oval holes *are stronger than round because they are narrow at the end grain*

ASYMMETRICAL PLATTERS

Placing the handle *at the side allows two platters to be cut from one billet*

Cut the curved shoulder *in the middle section for equal faces*

MAKE A
CHOPPING BOARD

Planing a solid wood chopping board is a sensible project to complete before embarking on joinery, since it teaches you how to create completely flat and true surfaces from which accurate measurements may be taken. As a bonus, you will end up with a beautiful and useful item for the kitchen!

YOU WILL NEED

TOOLS & EQUIPMENT

- Pencil and ruler or tape measure
- Work bench
- Bench stop
- Handsaw
- Scrub plane
- Winding sticks
- Jack plane
- Spare plywood
- Marking gauge
- Electric drill and 7mm (¼in) drill bit
- Frame saw
- Straight knife
- *optional*: F-clamp, vice, board gauge

MATERIALS

- Section of waney edge plank, avoiding end splits and areas of potential moisture damage
- Cardboard, for the handle template

SKILLS

YOU WILL LEARN TO

- Use planes: *steps 2–6, 8, 11*
- Measure from a datum: *steps 2–3, 5–8*
- Use a frame saw: *step 10*

REMIND YOURSELF HOW TO

- Correct wind: *p94*
- Use an electric drill: *p24*
- Carve a chamfered edge: *p16*

KNIFE GRIPS

- Thumb pivot: *p22*

DESIGN GUIDE

Apart from the practical elegance of the curved handle, the main design feature of the board lies in the tactile beauty of its planed surfaces.

Faces and sides *planed totally flat and straight to prevent rocking*

570mm (22⁷⁄₁₆in)

375mm (14³⁄₄in)

Handle for carrying *and hanging up in the kitchen*

Handle cut out *with a frame saw and chamfered with a straight knife*

30mm (1³⁄₁₆in)

Straight sides *chamfered with a plane*

OVERHEAD VIEW

66 TREAT THE JOB OF PLANING AS A CHANCE TO DRAW OUT THE TREMENDOUS BEAUTY TO BE FOUND IN WOOD GRAIN. 99

USING PLANES

Use your body to push behind your strongest arm with your other hand guiding. It is usually efficient to plane diagonally, overlapping cuts.

1. Scrub plane – Cuts thick shavings, useful for quickly roughing a flat surface. Maintain cuts in the same direction to take full length shavings.

2. Jack plane – This low-angled plane works well on end grain. An adjustable mouth can be reduced for the finest cuts. With its longer and wider sole it can be used for a "true" surface.

The Process

1 Rough cut to size

Mark and saw your boards roughly to size. For the greatest accuracy, sizing the boards will be done once the face has been planed flat. An edge is then accurately planed adjacent to it, and these two datum surfaces (face and edge) can be used for accurately marking out, something which is even more important for joinery projects.

Cut through the central slot in your work bench, if it has one

2 Select the datum side

If the board is very warped you may find that one side sits better on the work bench than the other. To hold the board in place, you can usually get away with just using a bench stop, but you may prefer to use an F-clamp as well. The first job is to rough the face with a scrub plane; note in the picture where the plane takes off the high points.

CUPPING

Planks are often cut tangentially out of logs – that is, not along the radius – and so tend to have the curved growth rings running horizontally through the plank. This can make planks prone to a type of warping called "cupping", caused by the annual growth rings attempting to flatten out as the wood dries.

Tangential cuts *feature curved grain*

PLANK SOURCE

Curves straighten *and cause cupping*

CUPPING EFFECT

Plane the surface *until entirely flat and smooth*

Look across *the top edges to see where the wood is warped*

3 Correct the wind

Scrub plane opposite ends to create reference points for winding sticks to help remove warp from the face of the board. Start in the corners and plane until you have cut the full width. Place winding sticks across the planed ends, and use them to identify where the bulk needs to be planed off.

Technique: Correcting wind – see p94

4 Smooth out the scallops

Correct the wind in the middle portion of the board. Switch to the jack plane to smooth over the scalloped surface left by the scrub, working cuts in the same direction. When trying to make a flat surface keep the sole of the plane flat on the board; when smoothing you may need to change the direction of cut depending on the grain direction. A finer plane called a smoothing plane may be used, but it is good practice to aim for a smooth surface from the jack.

CONTINUED ☞

TIP
You could use a vice or
F-clamp to fix the board
vertically to the work bench
so that you can plane the
sides horizontally.

5 Cut and plane face edge

Mark a pencil guideline for one of
the long sides of the board and saw
off the excess. Sawn surfaces are never
straight, however, and to create a totally
flat and square edge you need to true
the sawn side with the jack plane. Take
the opportunity to plane the sawn short
edges as well. By using the plane on its
side like this, you can use the flatness
on the work bench and the squareness
of the plane to make this cut at 90° to
the face; it is always worth checking
these things with a try square as well.

**Raise the
board** *on
plywood to
give clearance
for the plane*

6 Measure a parallel
from the edge

You have now created a datum
of one straight, flat long side from
which a parallel side can be marked.
A board gauge, shown here, is a useful
tool for marking the new parallel edge,
but definitely not necessary; a long
ruler, with measurements taken from
either end and joined together, will
suffice. Cut off the waste with a saw
or axe and plane smooth and flat. Now
you have two parallel sides, the ends
can be cut square. Use a try square and
marking knife to mark the square ends,
which can then be sawn off and planed
with the low angle jack plane.

The pencil marks *are shaved off when the face is level all over*

8 Plane down to the final thickness

Use the scrub then jack planes to cut a wide bevel on all sides of the board, planing down until you just reach the pencil line You can then colour in the new wide bevels with the pencil to give you a clear marker as to how far your planing has got. Keep going until you have a smooth and flat surface to the correct thickness of board.

7 Set the final thickness of the board

Examine the sides to identify where the wood is thinnest; this gives you the maximum thickness possible for a board with parallel flat faces. Set the marking gauge to this width and score a line all round, then highlight by running a pencil along the groove.

Press hard *on the gauge to score a line as deep as possible*

CONTINUED ☞

USING A FRAME SAW

The low number of teeth on a frame saw blade makes it ideal for cutting curves, as does the thinness of the blade, which facilitates turning.

To turn the blade, relieve the tension in the frame by loosening the string and then twist the blade fixing.

To cut internal hollows, detach the blade, insert it through a drilled hole, and reattach.

9 Mark on the handle

Make a card template for the handle hole. Mark a line on the template at the midpoint, and an equivalent line down the midpoint of the board. Determine how wide to make the handle and draw a horizontal guideline for the base of the hole. Draw round the template, then draw the curves of the handle freehand.

A handle width of at least 40mm (1⁹⁄₁₆in) is advisable for strength

10 Saw the handle

Drill a 7mm (¼in) starter hole for the frame saw, close to the top of the midpoint of the handle hole, then thread through the blade; *see* Using a frame saw, above. Roughly cut out the shape of the hole, leaving a thin margin of waste next to the pencil line. Then roughly saw the top curve of the handle.

Technique: Using an electric drill – see p24

Do not saw right along or up to the guideline – leave waste for finer knife cuts

Support your knife *hand for strength and stability*

Design variations

A few simple adaptations transform the basic design into a cheese or carving board. If you cut a hole into one end of the cheese board, you could fit the wire using a second toggle.

CHEESE BOARD

Wire pinned *or screwed to side*

Chisel a central groove *to let the wire cut through*

Carve a toggle *for the handle*

CARVING BOARD

Hole *in the handle for easy storage*

Edge groove *for catching meat juices*

Cut the groove *with a gouge, drilling depth holes in the corners as guides*

11 Refine the handle and chamfer edges

Finish cutting the handle with a straight knife, using thumb pivot grip to cut to the pencil line. Alternatively, if the board is still clamped you can use the knife in two hands working away from yourself. Resting your arms on the board and pivoting your body around the cut, you can safely refine the curve. Try to create smooth curved edges, refine the sawn surfaces, and cut a chamfer along all of the handle edges. Finally, use a jack plane to cut a chamfer along each of the straight edges of the board.

Knife grip: Thumb pivot – see p22

Technique: Carving a chamfered edge – see p16

Tilt the plane *to cut an angled chamfer*

MAKE A
Shrink Pot

The genius of this pot lies – as the name suggests – in the shrinking. The lid and base pieces are split out first, roughly shaped, and left to dry. The cylindrical main body of the pot is then shaped from green wood and fitted to the dry pieces, which allows the sides of the pot to shrink in naturally to fix the base in position.

YOU WILL NEED

TOOLS & EQUIPMENT

- Mallets, large and small
- Froe
- Pencil, compass, and ruler
- Bench hook
- Handsaw (such as a pull saw)
- Straight knife
- Axe
- Work bench
- Auger
- Measuring gauge
- Electric drill and 8mm ($\frac{5}{16}$in) drill bit
- *optional:* 180 grit abrasive paper

MATERIALS

- 1 green wood log, around 175mm (6⅞in) in both length and diameter, for the lid, knob, and base
- 1 green wood log, around 80mm (3⅛in) in both length and diameter, for the pot cylinder
- Offcut, for the wedge

SKILLS

YOU WILL LEARN TO

- Form a tenon and mortise joint with wedge: *steps 11–15*

REMIND YOURSELF HOW TO

- Split with a froe: *p82*
- Use a pull saw: *p24*
- Baton with a knife: *p16*
- Correct wind: *p94*
- True with an axe: *p94*
- Use an auger: *p30*
- Use an electric drill: *p24*
- Carve a chamfered edge: *p16*

KNIFE GRIPS

- Thumb pull: *p21*
- Chest lever: *p19*
- Wrist twist: *p112*
- Pencil grip: *p28*
- Reinforced pull: *p32*
- Thumb push: *p22*
- Thumb pivot: *p22*

DESIGN GUIDE

The size of your shrink pot need only be limited by the size of the log from which you shape the cylinder. It is sensible, however, to start with a small one, which will open the door to lots of possibilities. This size pot would be perfect for storing salt or sugar, or for keeping small trinkets in.

Knob fitted *with a wedged tenon and mortise*

Lid tapers *to fit the rim, which tapers into the body of the pot*

Cylinder shrinks *around the base*

75mm (2¹⁵⁄₁₆in)

Angled groove *for fitting the base disc*

Dry base disc *inserted into green wood cylinder*

78mm (3in)

EXPLODED VIEW

> **USING A QUARTERSAWN PLANK** MEANS THE LID AND BASE WILL **SHRINK** WITH A **MINIMAL** AMOUNT OF **CUPPING.**

TIP
Rough shaping the lid and removing the bark helps speed up the drying process by exposing more end grain.

The Process

Use one half for the lid and knob, and split the other for the base

1 Split out billets
With a mallet and froe, split out a plank 20mm (¾in) thick. Take it from the middle of the log, where, viewed end on, the growth rings run perpendicular to the plank. Split the plank in half down the middle. Then split one of these halves lengthways.

Technique: Splitting with a froe – see p82

2 Rough shape the lid
At one end of the wider billet, mark a circle guideline with a diameter of 78mm (3in), for the lid. Mark the straight sides of an octagon around the circle, then cut out the octagon with a saw. Tidy and rough shape with a knife, but leave the lid oversized to allow for shrinkage.

Technique: Using a pull saw – see p24

Knife grip: Thumb pull – see p21

Use thumb pull grip *to tidy up the sides and remove bark*

3 Shape the knob billet

Take the remaining half of the wider billet and use a knife and mallet to baton out a rectangular bit of wood for the knob, roughly square in cross section. Use chest lever grip to shave the sides to a true square: sight the billet end on for twists, then shave two adjoining surfaces flat and square, from which you can true the other two surfaces.

Technique: Batoning with a knife – see p16

Knife grip: Chest lever – see p19

4 Flatten the base billet

Create flat parallel sides to the base billet by shaving it down slightly with an axe. Sight along the billet for where there are any twists in the grain – known as "wind" – and even these out by taking shavings from one side. Leave these three pieces to dry for up to three weeks.

Techniques: Correcting wind, Truing with an axe – see p94

Use a shallow, gentle action *to take thin shavings from the midpoint*

CONTINUED ☞

WRIST TWIST GRIP

Check to see if the tip of the knife blade will poke through the bottom; if it does, take extra care to avoid cutting yourself.

Wrap your fingers around the handle of the knife and effect the cut by pushing the knife with the heel of your palm.

As you push the knife, twist the billet in the opposite direction; you are following the growth rings, and can therefore cut all the way round in the same direction.

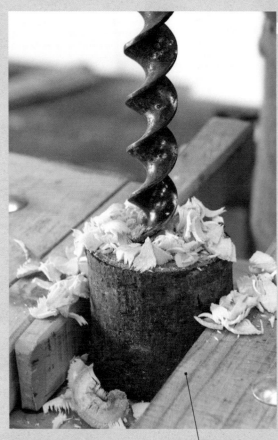

5 Cut a hole for the cylinder

Take the log for the cylinder and secure it on a work bench. You could do this with wedges against uprights; or alternatively, use a vice, F-clamp, or your feet. Centre the auger and bore in until a hole is cut clean through the log.

Technique: Using an auger – see p30

Wedging the log *between uprights is one way to secure it*

6 Expand the hole

Shave out the rest of the waste wood with a knife, down to a thickness of 8mm (⁵⁄₁₆in), using a wrist twist action; *see* above. Shorter shavings are easier to take, so carve out half of the pot at a time, approaching from either end in turn. Shave off the bark with chest lever grip, then use thumb pull to true the base. For larger cylinders, an incannel gouge could be used, or a series of connected smaller drill holes, or the frame saw with a good blade.

Shave the base *of the pot to a flat surface*

Cut the outer half first *so that you can grip the other end of the billet*

TIP

Ensure the base fits fairly loosely at this stage, since a tight fit could result in the wood splitting as the cylinder shrinks.

7 Cut the groove

Mark a short pencil line inside the pot, 12mm (½in) up from the base. Set a marking gauge to this depth, tighten the screw, and score a deep line all the way round, then score a second line 3mm (⅛in) nearer the base. Chip out the wood between these lines with the point of a knife. The groove should be 4 or 5mm (³⁄₁₆in) deep; if it is too shallow, the cylinder may split upon shrinking. Cut the groove flat at the top edge and bevelled at the bottom.

Knife grip: Pencil grip – see p28

Grip the blade *along the blunt top, like a pencil*

8 Shape and fit the base

Place the cylinder at one end of the base billet and draw a guideline around the inside edge. Cut out along this line for the outer half of the disc, using chest lever grip then thumb pull for finer cuts close to the line. Mark another rounded line 12mm (½in) further in, and cut a chamfer to this line. Repeat the process on the opposite side, switching to reinforced grip; leave a small section of excess wood attached to make chamfering the last section easier – then saw it off and refine with a knife. Pop in the base, making sure one side is held in the groove, then leave the pot to shrink over a couple of weeks.

Knife grip: Reinforced pull – see p32

Insert the base *with the chamfered side facing out*

CONTINUED ☞

SETTING THE TAPER

To determine the gradient of the taper on your lid (and rim), you can either decide to cut in by Y amount over X distance (X being the thickness of the lid); or you can pick an angle of gradient, and use a sliding bevel to mark that angle and guide your tapering cuts.

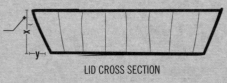

For a shallow gradient , *opt for a relatively narrow angle or width*

LID CROSS SECTION

Shape and taper *the lid using thumb pull grip*

9 Shape the lid

Place the pot top-down on the lid piece and draw round it, then shape to this guideline. Decide on the taper gradient; a shallow gradient is good for a lid. There are two ways to achieve the gradient; *see* Setting the taper, above. We chose to taper the lid down to a specific width, marked with a circular pencil guideline.

10 Refine the rim

To fit the lid, an entirely circular edge to the rim of the pot helps a great deal. Find something round, if need be, to draw on a guideline, and shave the outside edge to this line using thumb pull grip. Switch to the wrist twist to taper the inside rim to match the gradient of the lid. If you are struggling with the fit, wrap some 180 grit abrasive paper around the lid and use it to abrade the mortise to the correct shape.

Taper fairly straight *at the rim, and blend in gradually down the pot*

TIP

The knob billet may have warped as it dried. Check if it is still square and make adjustments with the knife, if required.

> ❝ FOR A **TIGHT FIT**, MAKE THE **TENON** A FRACTION **WIDER** THAN THE **MORTISE**, ESPECIALLY IF USING **SOFTER WOOD**. ❞

12 Rough shape the tenon

Saw to the required depth along the tenon length guidelines on each face. Use a knife in thumb push grip to pare away the waste material around the tenon, and the reinforced pull stroke to cut back down to the saw kerf. Cut to the square guideline, then further refine the shape of the tenon down to an octagon.

Knife grip: Thumb push – see p22

Take off the corners *of the sawn sides to further shape the tenon*

11 Mark the tenon

Mark a centre line on each of the long faces of the knob billet, then use these lines to help you draw a square in the centre of one of the ends, for the shape of the tenon. Next mark a horizontal guideline all the way round the billet to the length of the tenon. Measure how far in from the edge of the billet the tenon will sit, and stick tape on the saw blade at this distance, to act as a guide for how deep to cut.

CONTINUED ☞

FOCUS ON...
WEDGED TENON JOINT

Fitting a wedge into a tenon helps achieve a tight fit to the joint, which is especially important if you are using softer wood. To begin with, you should aim for the tenon to be ever so slightly larger than the mortise. Inserting a relatively thick wedge then forces apart the sides of tenon, so that the wood fibres of the tenon and mortise compress against each other.

A "kerf" line *is sawn into the tenon*

Tapered wedge *spreads the tenon for a secure fit*

The shape *of the knob resembles the capital of a Doric column*

13 Cut the slot and shape the knob

Saw straight down the centre of the tenon to create the slot for the wedge. Shape the knob by first drawing a guideline 5mm (¼in) short of its full height, then shaving off the corners from this line down to the tenon, using thumb pivot grip. Next shave down the flat faces, working eight sides but leaving it square at the top. Mark another guideline 5mm (¼in) beyond the first, and saw off the waste at this point.

Knife grip: Thumb pivot – see p22

Mark the width *of the mortise on the wedge billet*

14 Drill the mortise and cut a wedge

Drill an 8mm (⁵⁄₁₆in) mortise hole for the knob tenon, positioning it slightly off-centre; this way the knob will open the lid more efficiently. Baton the billet down to size with a knife and taper it to a thin ridge to form the wedge. Test fit the tenon, shaving off waste if needed, then insert.

Technique: Using an electric drill – p24

Tap the wedge *with the head of an axe or small mallet*

A thick *chamfer looks attractive*

15 Tap in the wedge

Insert the tenon into the mortise. Make a mark on the wedge at two-thirds of the thickness of the lid. Tap the wedge into the tenon slot up to this mark, then use a pull saw to remove the majority of the protruding waste. For a stronger joint, glue could be used on the tenon; glue only one side of the wedge, to allow for movement of the wedge.

16 Finish shaping the lid and knob

Use a knife in thumb pull grip to tidy up the remaining waste at the end of the tenon. Cut a chamfer around the top edge of the lid. Finally, shape the top of the knob by bringing the four sides to a point, and then chamfer the square edge.

Technique: Carving a chamfered edge – see p16

Design variations

Tapering the sides of the lid and pot rim is only one way to achieve a tight fit. Other options include creating a lip to the lid, or cutting slots in the side of the cylinder so that the lid sits flush.

SOLID LIPPED LID

Lid fits *by way of a lip, cut to match the width of the cylinder rim*

Reduce the bulk *of the solid lid by hollowing out the base*

TWO-PIECE LIPPED LID

Fitting principle *is the same as for the solid lid, but simpler to achieve*

The lip is made *by gluing together two discs of wood*

SLOTTED LID

Two opposite *wedges form a bow-tie shape*

Matching slots *are sawn into the cylinder*

MAKE A
FRAME SAW

The thin blade of a frame saw is good for curved cuts and reduces friction, and being interchangeable you can choose the best blade for the task at hand. Making one is a great way to practise joinery – mark out precisely, and you will end up with a staple tool.

YOU WILL NEED

TOOLS & EQUIPMENT
- Jack plane
- Measuring equipment
- Pull saw
- Mallet and chisels: 8mm (⁵⁄₁₆in) and 16mm (⁵⁄₈in)
- Clamps and spare plywood
- Straight knife
- Auger
- Hacksaw or angle grinder and safety goggles
- Metal file and metal pliers
- Electric drill, 2mm (¹⁄₁₆in) metal bit, and centre punch
- Lighter

- Froe, axe, and axeblock
- *optional:* Plane stop, marking knife

MATERIALS
- 3 green wood planks, split out and trued to around 37mm (1½in) wide and 21mm (⅞in) thick; *see pp82 and 94*
- 1 green wood log, around 40mm (1⅝in) in diameter, for the wedge
- Bandsaw blade, at least 570mm (22⁷⁄₁₆in) long
- 2 x 2mm (¹⁄₁₆in) nails
- Strong, inflexible string, e.g. starter cord for a motor, at least 1.2m (3ft 11in) long

SKILLS

YOU WILL LEARN TO
- Form a mortise-and-tenon joint – *steps 4–7*
- Use a chisel – *steps 4–7, 10–11*
- Use a marking knife – *step 5*

REMIND YOURSELF HOW TO
- Use a plane – *p100*
- Measure from a datum – *p94*
- Use a pull saw – *p24*
- Use an auger – *p30*
- Split with a froe – *p82*

KNIFE GRIPS
- Thumb pull, push – *pp21, 22*
- Reinforced pull – *p32*

DESIGN GUIDE

The frame that gives the saw its name is constructed from three lengths of wood. There should be enough space between the blade and cross bar for you to hold the saw comfortably.

Hooked tops *to arms hold the string*

Wedge used *to twist string taut*

Tightened string *places frame and blade under tension*

Mortise-and-tenon *joints hold frame together*

Recessed edges *provide handles for gripping*

475mm (18¹¹⁄₁₆in)

540mm (21¼in)

Saw blade *held in place with pins*

FRONT VIEW

TIP
You'll know a surface is
flat if you are able to take a
full-length and -width
shaving off the surface
with the plane.

**The mirror
surface** *will show
if you are tilting
the saw*

The Process

1 Shave the planks parallel

Shave one of the wide
faces of a plank to a flat
datum with a jack plane.
Set a measuring gauge from
this datum and mark a line for
the thickness, taken from the
thinnest point. Emphasise the
line with a sharp, hard pencil,
and plane down to this line to
form two parallel surfaces.

**Techniques: Using a plane,
measuring from a datum
– see p98**

Mark the datum
*face side and edge
to measure from*

2 Saw the planks square

Repeat the planing process for
the thinner faces, and then do
the same for the other planks. Now
saw the planks to size, making sure
you cut totally square by marking
guidelines on two faces with a try
square and keeping the pull saw
straight. A good trick is to polish
the saw surface to act as a mirror
for sighting; the reflection should
line up perfectly with the board.

**Technique: Using a pull saw
– see p24**

1. Delicate vertical chops set the sides of the mortise and form a "shoulder" to work from. Centre the chisel with your fingers before each cut, and sight against a try square to keep it vertical.

2. Tilt the chisel to lever out chips. First clear a deep V-notch in the centre of the mortise, to create space to take out bigger chips and allow them to split along the grain.

3 Draw the mortise hole

Mark out the mortise on an arm piece, starting the bottom at the halfway point and making it the same size as the tenon. Draw the top and bottom lines, then mark the mortise hole with a marking gauge. Set the width of the mortise with the mortise chisel, in this case 8mm (⁵⁄₁₆in); it should be around one-third of the plank thickness. Score the side of the mortise using a marking gauge, measuring from the face. The plank is 20mm (¹³⁄₁₆in) thick, so set the gauge to 6mm (¼in).

The gauge *severs the first layer of fibres of the mortise*

4 Chisel the mortise

Chop out the mortise with a mallet and 8mm (⁵⁄₁₆in) chisel; *see* above. First make a series of shallow vertical cuts, starting from the middle and ending 2mm (¹⁄₁₆in) shy of the end, so that you can remove the wood without damaging the edge of the mortise. Take the cuts deeper until you reach a depth of 25mm (1in). Pare the waste from the ends, lining up the chisel blade exactly with the edge line. Repeat steps 3 and 4 on the second arm.

CONTINUED ☞

USING A MARKING KNIFE

I. Hold the ruler still with one hand and press in the tip of the knife. Keep the knife still in the wood and remove the ruler.

2. Slide the try square along the edge until it rests against the knife. Hold the square still and score a square line.

Continue the guideline around each face by placing the knife in the corner groove left by the previous line, and butting it against the try square.

5 Mark the tenon

Mark out a tenon at the end of the cross piece. Set the tenon length to 25mm (1in) and score a guideline on all faces with a marking knife; *see* above. To mark the tenon width, score a centre line, lightly push in the chisel centred on this line, then set the gauge to the edges of the chisel mark and score round the faces.

6 Saw the tenon

Clamp the piece securely and saw two depth lines, keeping the blade straight, then saw along the grain; a tenon saw or ripsaw would work well for this. Saw diagonally along the two lines at once, tackling them from both sides, before finally sawing straight down to the shoulder.

Chisel a notch
along each scored line to help align the saw

TIP

Chamfering the end of the tenon helps it to fit in the mortise, and prevents mistakes arising from a "flaring" tenon.

Use a try square to help you drill straight down

Remove material *where the tenon is sticking*

7 Chamfer and test the fit

Chamfer the ends of the tenon with a knife in thumb pull grip. Test the fit in the mortise: if it is too wide, pare back the cheeks with a wide chisel to keep the surface true. If both corners fit but it won't go in straight, you may need to reduce the tenon width; do this on just one side, and if needed on the other end of the cross piece make sure you do it from the same edge.

Technique: Carving a chamfered edge – see p16

Knife grip: Thumb pull – see p21

8 Form the saw slot

At the handle end of an arm piece, mark centre and depth guidelines for the saw blade slot, which should be deep enough for the blade to sit entirely within it. Saw the slot as you did the tenons. Drill a hole for the blade pin, positioning it centrally to give the pin strength against splitting the arm under tension in use. Repeat on the other arm.

CONTINUED ☞

TIP
The more stop cuts, the more work with the saw – but the easier it will be to chisel out the waste.

9 Start to shape the crook

Draw the "shepherd's crook" shape at the top of an arm piece, making sure the curve is on the opposite side to the mortise, so that it points outwards. Drill a hole with an auger at the inside edge of the hook; a great way to get a tight curve where the string will wrap round. Mark a cross, clamp to a bit of plywood, and drill straight through.

**Technique: Using an auger
– see p30**

10 Saw stop cuts

Remove the remaining waste with a saw and chisel. First, use a pencil and try square to draw a series of perpendicular guidelines along the slope of the crook, marking both faces and stopping just short of the sloping guideline. Saw down each of these lines to create "stop cuts" where the chisel edge will come to rest, helping to control the chiselling action.

Don't saw beyond the *guideline – you will tidy it up later*

" AS WELL AS LOOKING ELEGANT, THE CHAMFERED AND CONVEX SURFACE TO THE HOOK PREVENTS THE STRING FROM FRAYING AGAINST THE CORNERS OF THE WOOD. "

The arms
*should be
mirror images
in shape*

12 Refine the hook

Return to the knife to further shape the crook. Employ thumb pull or thumb push grips to cut concave chamfers underneath, starting from a little way up the slope and pinching into the hook slightly, then to refine the top curve and chamfer the edges. Switch to reinforced grip to cut a straight, thick chamfer down the edges of the rest of the slope. Repeat steps 9–12 on the other arm.

Knife grip: Thumb push – see p22

You may need
*to go over the
area a few
times to remove
all of the waste*

11 Chisel the slope

Starting at the shallow end of the slope, chip out the waste with a mallet and chisel, then tidy the chiselled surface with a knife in reinforced pull grip. Begin to shape the top of the crook by sawing off the corners.

Knife grip: Reinforced pull – see p32

CONTINUED ☞

Make the
recesses
8–10mm
(⁵⁄₁₆–³⁄₈in)
deep

**Hold the
blade** *over
the end of a
work bench*

13 Form the handle grips

Mark rectangular guidelines
on each face of the arm for the four
recesses of each handle grip,
indicating the depth of the concave
and where the curve will start and
finish. Cut each recess, first
removing a notch at either end to
the depth of the concave using the
thumb push grip, then shaving down
the waste between with reinforced
pull. Chamfer all edges, then repeat
on the other arm.

14 Cut the saw blade

Put on safety goggles, and
use a hacksaw or angle
grinder to cut the band saw blade to
the correct length. Leave the blade a
little long, so that the frame can bow
out slightly when the blade is nailed
in place, which helps create tension.
Remove any sharp corners from the
ends of the blade with a metal file.

> POSITIONING THE SECOND PIN SHORT MEANS THE FRAME WILL BE SLIGHTLY OFFSET, AND HENCE REMAIN FAIRLY SQUARE UNDER TENSION.

15 Drill a pin hole

Assemble the frame, then insert the saw blade to the correct depth, ends flush with the arm edges. Mark the spot for the pin hole by "tickling" it with the electric drill and metal bit, then remove the blade from the arm. Clamp the blade on scrap wood, hammer a centre punch on the mark, and, wearing safety goggles, drill the hole.

16 Drill second hole and pin saw

Measure between the centres of the pin holes on the frame, and subtract 3mm (⅛in) to give you the position of the second drill point. Mark with a pen, then centrepunch and drill, as before. Test fit the nails for pinning the blades, clip them to size with metal pliers, and file off any sharp edges. Pin the blade in place.

Clip the waste *so that the nail is flush with the frame*

CONTINUED ☞

DOUBLE FISHERMAN'S KNOT

I. Place the two ends of the string side by side. Loosely wind both ends twice around the other to form two loops. If you wound the first end over the other string, wind the second end under the first.

2. Pull the ends back through the two loops to tighten, then pull them again to bring the two parts of the knot together.

Pull the longer ends *of the string to slide the knots together*

I.

2.

The loop *should be slack enough to take off, but still under tension*

17 Fit the string

Wrap the string around the hooks of the arms and cut to length, leaving 100mm (3¹⁵⁄₁₆in) of slack for tying the knot. Tie the ends together with a double fisherman's knot; *see above*. Fuse the ends by melting them with a lighter, so that they don't fray and unravel.

18 Form the wedge

Split out a billet for the wedge, around 250mm (9¹³⁄₁₆in) long, 35mm (1⁷⁄₁₆in) wide, and 16mm (⅝in) thick, taking it from a tangent rather than radius of the log, for strength. Chop off the bark with an axe and shape it into a wedge with a slight taper at one end. Use a knife and reinforced pull stroke to remove any sharp edges, then chamfer the top and bottom with thumb pull grip.

Technique: Splitting with a froe – p82

Design variations

We have opted for a simple slot and pin method of fitting the blade. Here are a couple of options for alternative fixings that, while much more complicated, allow the blade to be rotated.

SPLIT PIN

Split pin *can be turned to adjust blade angle*

Saw blade

Looped bolt *fixed on arm with a washer*

Pin holds *the saw blade to the bolt*

WOODEN HANDLES

Handle held *tight when frame is under tension*

Blade pinned *in slot sawn into knob*

Handle fitted *to frame in a reamed hole*

19 Fit the wedge

To place the saw under tension, start to twist the string with your fingers until a slot appears in the middle. Insert the wedge into the slot and use it to twist the string further, until the saw is under a lot of tension: ping the blade and you should be able to hear when it has changed key. Leave the saw untensioned when not in use, otherwise you will stretch the blade.

> ❝ LEAVE THE SAW UNTENSIONED WHEN NOT IN USE, TO AVOID STRETCHING THE BLADE. ❞

MAKE A
FRAME STOOL

This project explores the tensile properties of wood, and provides an introduction to post and rung joinery, a simple and adaptable style of furniture making. The seat is woven from the discarded rubber inner tubes of bicycles, a resource that may otherwise go to landfill, and results in a very comfortable sitting experience.

YOU WILL NEED

TOOLS & EQUIPMENT

- Measuring equipment
- Knife and small log or mallet
- Marking gauge
- Large and small froes, large mallet
- Shaving horse and draw knife
- 9.5mm (⅜in) tapered tenon cutter
- Try square
- Work bench
- Bench hook
- Pull saw
- 2 large F-clamps
- Spare thin pieces of wood
- Hammer and nail
- Electric drill with 6mm (¼in) and 5mm (³⁄₁₆in) bits

- 9.5mm (⅜in) reamer
- Marker pen
- Paintbrush
- PVA glue
- *optional*: Compass or dividers, cleaving brake

MATERIALS

- 1 or more green wood logs, around 600mm (23⅝in) long
- Smaller, dry piece of the same wood, at least 50 x 18 x 9mm (2 x ¾ x ⅜in), for the pegs
- Plank of "2 x 4"
- Old bicycle inner tubes (often available free from bike shops); cleaned, valves cut off, and rough patches sanded smooth

SKILLS

YOU WILL LEARN TO

- Use a tenon cutter: *step 11*
- Make a jig: *step 13*
- Use a reamer: *step 15*
- Peg joints: *steps 18–19*

REMIND YOURSELF HOW TO

- Baton with a knife: *p16*
- Split with a froe: *p82*
- Use a draw knife: *p94*
- Correct wind: *p94*
- Form a tapered tenon: *p56*
- Use a pull saw: *p24*
- Use an electric drill: *p24*
- Level legs: *p154*

KNIFE GRIPS

- Thumb pull: *p21*
- Thumb pivot: *p22*

DESIGN GUIDE

The stool follows a basic frame design using long and short rungs set at different heights. The joints need to be very strong to resist the high degree of torque (twisting force) created by the woven inner tubes. Tapered tenons are a lot stronger than straight tenons, and are given additional strength by being glued and pegged. Note that the rung measurements shown include the lengths of the tenons.

500mm (19¹¹⁄₁₆in)

300mm (11¹³⁄₁₆in)

460mm (18⅛in)

3D VIEW

Tops of legs *cut as short as possible to prevent them digging into thighs*

Even rung spacing *gives the structure strength*

Make rungs *the right height to rest feet on*

> **TAPERED JOINTS** ARE STRONG AND **ELEGANT**.
> IT IS IMPORTANT THAT THE **TENONS LINE UP** ON EITHER END
> OF EACH **RUNG** TO AVOID **GAPS** AROUND THE **MORTISES**,
> SO MEASURE **ACCURATELY**.

The Process

1 Make 16 pegs

Saw a small, dry billet to around 50mm (2in) long. Split this billet into 9 x 9mm (⅜ x ⅜in) sections, then split one of those in half and half again to create four pegs around 4.5mm (³⁄₁₆in) wide. A marking gauge is helpful for measuring out these pegs. In total you will need 16. Chamfer both ends of each peg using thumb pivot grip.

Technique: Batoning with a knife – see p16

Knife grips: Thumb pull, thumb pivot – see pp21, 22

2 Mark and split the log

Split out billets for four legs, 40mm (1⁹⁄₁₆in) in diameter, and two long rungs and four short rungs, each 26mm (1in) in diameter. Plan a cleaving strategy to make the most efficient use of the wood. Mark the components to see how they might split out; a compass or dividers can be useful. Using a large mallet and froe, split the log in half and half again, then into two quarter wedges, along the line. If you need to split the wood into thirds, do this early on, leaving the majority of cleaving as simple halving.

Technique: Splitting with a froe – see p82

Push with your knee *and lever the sides apart with the froe*

Cleaving brakes hold the end of a piece of wood as you split it, and help to control the split. By levering against the cleaving brake you are able to pry apart the wood and apply strain to the chosen side of the split.

Place the wood into the middle of the brake with the bottom end pointing away from you. The side of the billet that you want the split to run towards should always be facing down; when you push down on the froe, you will create tension where it is needed.

TIP
Hold the leg against the side of your shaving horse to check for straightness.

3 Split out legs and rungs
For the finer divisions, use a smaller mallet and froe and, if you have one, a cleaving brake; *see* above. Put tension on the thicker side (if there is one) by pushing down on the froe blade, then levering the split open with your elbow against the handle of the froe, pulling it towards you. Without a cleaving brake, the wood can be cleaved against the ground with the thin side down. If the split starts running off, flip the billet around and put pressure on the other side to control it.

Ignore the circles *at this point and split the wood down the middle, as accurately as you can*

4 Start shaping a leg
Take a leg billet and use a draw knife on a shaving horse to create a straight datum, from which the other sides can be measured. Set the datum on the bark side, since the outside of a tree tends to have more tension than the inside, and the wood is likely to be more bowed. Start by taking short shavings off the ends of the billet, then work your way in towards the centre – at the very centre you may only need to skim off the bark. Flip it round to work the other half.

Techniques: Using a draw knife, correcting wind – see p94

CONTINUED ☞

> **THE GROWTH RINGS** ON A BILLET SUCH AS THIS CAN ACT LIKE **CONTOUR LINES** ON A MAP – REMOVE THE HILLS TO CREATE A **FLAT SURFACE** WITH PARALLEL LINES. **"**

Shave down in three facets, *taking off the corners, rather than trying to take single wide shavings*

5 Square a leg billet

With a pencil, mark out a 45mm (1³⁄₄in) square at one end of a leg billet, measuring from the datum. Your piece of wood may well be wedge-shaped rather than cuboid, so adjust your cuts accordingly. Make sure this side is straight all the way down; rest the billet against the side of the shaving horse to gauge where material needs to be removed. Repeat on the remaining two sides, so that the cross-section of your leg is square.

6 Make the square leg octagonal

Clamp the leg at 45° and shave off the corner to create a new flat facet. Work around the whole leg, shaving off each corner so the square ends become octagonal. Widen the corner facets and shave off more material, until all eight faces are parallel and the same width.

7 Shave to a cylinder

Now turn the octagonal leg into a cylinder by taking off each corner. You do not need to shave off much wood here; thin shavings off each corner will create a rounded shape. Continue working on the leg until it is smooth. Repeat steps 3–6 to make three more identical legs, then make eight rungs in the same way; each should be around 25mm (1in) in diameter. Saw the rungs to size.

Keep the shavings
thin and in long curls

8 Mark tenons on the rungs

Draw a cross on the end of a rung, as close to the centre as possible; this will help you cut the tenon straight. Measure 80mm (3⅛in) down from the end and draw a ring around the rung. The tenon will taper to an 8mm (⁵⁄₁₆in) point along this length. However, the wood will shrink before you assemble the chair, so at this stage you should make the end of the tenon slightly larger, at 12mm (½in) wide. Draw a 12mm (½in) diameter circle over the centre of the cross, for guidance.

CONTINUED ☞

TIP

The more you skew a draw knife the better the accuracy – if it is totally skewed, it will cut a straight line.

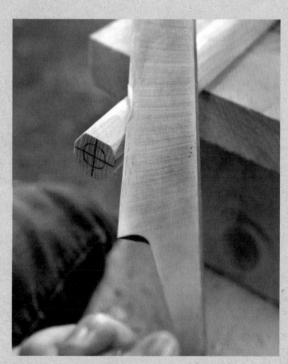

9 Start tapering the tenon

To shape the tenon, start the taper with a draw knife, taking off short shavings on one side of the rung. Begin at the tip of the tenon, where you need to take off more material, then work your way back to the line little by little.

Technique: Forming a tapered tenon – see p56

10 Rough shape the tenon end

Use the same square–octagon–circle technique shown in steps 5–7 to shape the end of the tenon, creating an even square first before taking off the corners to form a cone. Use the pencil circle as a guide, but leave a little waste to be finished with the tenon cutter.

Take care *not to make the surface of the tenon concave*

> **TAPERED TENONS ARE FAIRLY FORGIVING**: IF YOU SHAVE OFF **TOO MUCH**, THE TENON WILL SIMPLY **TRAVEL FURTHER** INTO THE MORTISE, AND **WEDGE** JUST AS **TIGHTLY**. **"**

11 Shape further with a tenon cutter

Place a 9.5mm (⅜in) tenon cutter onto the end of your tenon, aligning it centrally; the gap between the wood and cutter should be even all the way round. Hold the cutter in your non-dominant hand and twist the rung clockwise to shave off material, exactly like using a pencil sharpener. At this point, only use the tenon cutter on the first half of the tenon, to allow for shrinkage. Repeat steps 8–11 on both ends of all eight rungs.

Centre the tenon then focus on the widest part

12 Finish the tenons once dry

Leave the rungs to dry for 2–3 weeks, then work on them again with the tenon cutter, shaving material off until each tenon reaches the pencil line. You may need to use a draw knife to skim off any slight shoulders around the last third of each tenon first. The end points of these tenons should now measure 9.5mm (⅜in) in diameter. It is important that the rungs are the correct length, and that the tenons taper by the same amount; if one rung is too short, you will either have to remake it, or shorten all the other rungs to match it.

CONTINUED ☞

MAKING A JIG

A jig is the name given to a custom-made tool designed to hold items in place, so that they can be worked on safely and efficiently. The round legs of the stool would be liable to roll about on the work bench, and are difficult to clamp. This jig provides a rest for the legs to lie in, and makes it possible to clamp them securely and work on them together.

Offcut placed *over the legs to give a surface for clamping*

15mm (⁹⁄₁₆in)   15mm (⁹⁄₁₆in)   15mm (⁹⁄₁₆in)

25mm (1in)

50mm (1¹⁵⁄₁₆in)   50mm (1¹⁵⁄₁₆in)

Recesses *sized to make a secure but comfortable fit*

13 Make jigs to hold the legs

You will need to make two jigs in order to clamp the legs. Measure 145mm (5¹¹⁄₁₆in) from the end of a "2 x 4" plank and mark it with a pencil line. Then, using a set square for accuracy, mark out the measurements shown in the diagram above. Secure the plank on your work bench with bench hook, and use a pull saw to cut out triangular areas for the stool legs to lie in. Saw off the jig at the 145mm (5¹¹⁄₁₆in) line.

Technique: Using a pull saw – see p24

14 Drill holes in the legs

Place two legs in the jigs, on your work bench. Make two pencil crosses on each leg, at 38mm (1½in) and 240mm (9½in) from the top, sighting down the legs and using a ruler to ensure they are exactly central. Clamp the legs to the bench using an F-clamp and a small offcut. Drill holes at the crosses with a 6mm (¼in) drill bit, sighting with a try square to keep them straight.

Technique: Using an electric drill – see p24

Lightly tap on *a nail to make a centrepunch for the drill bit*

It is much easier *to shorten the tenons than to extend the mortises*

15 Ream the holes

Now taper the mortises to match the tenons; it is important to get the right depth to the holes at this point. The maximum width of the hole should be 17mm ($^{11}\!/_{16}$in), so find the point where the reaming attachment is at this width and mark it with a pen: this is the depth you need to ream to. Now ream down until the mark is aligned with the highest point of the edge of the hole. Reamers have very sharp cutting edges: make sure the pieces are secure, and keep the blades well clear of fingers!

Ream straight down *until the pen mark is level with the top of the wood*

16 Check the measurements

Once you have reamed all eight holes, dry fit the side panels and check that they match. Make sure the tenons are fully fitted to the reamed mortises, and check that the legs are parallel. If they are not, you need to shorten one or more of the rungs. Measure the length of each rung from the outside edges of the legs: they should all be the same length. If you have rungs of different lengths, find the shortest one and use the tenon cutter to adjust the other rungs to match it, checking them continually as you go.

CONTINUED ☛

CLAMPING THE PANELS

Two large F-clamps are needed to keep the side panel secure and held together tightly until the joints are pegged.

One clamp squeezes the legs and rungs together, while the other fixes the panel to the bench and holds it true and flat.

An offcut of wood placed over the middle of the rungs enables the panel to be held evenly in place by the second clamp.

17 Glue the tenons

Apply a small amount of PVA glue to the inside of each mortise in one of the two side panels, swizzling the brush round for an even coating. Fit the rungs, then clamp the side tightly to hold everything in place while you insert the pegs; *see* above.

18 Drill holes for the pegs

Mark a cross on each leg, centred on the tenon and one-third of the tenon depth in from the inside edge of the leg. Centrepunch the mark with a nail and hammer, then drill straight down all the way through the leg, using a 5mm (^{3}⁄$_{16}$in) drill bit. Start by drilling at an angle, towards the centre of the leg, to avoid the drill bit scooting off the curve; then quickly shift to drilling straight down, avoiding bending the drill bit.

> 66 HAVING THE FRONT AND REAR RUNGS LOWER CREATES A SLIGHT CURVE IN THE SEAT, MAKING IT MORE COMFORTABLE. 99

19 Hammer in the pegs

Lubricate each peg with some glue on the end third, before hammering it in square to the stool; the tapered ends of the pegs should come out the other side. Use a knife in thumb pull grip to remove the ends of the pegs where they stick out. Repeat steps 17–19 on the other panel.

Knife grip: Thumb pull – see p21

Shave down *the protruding peg ends flush to the leg*

20 Assemble the front and back

Choose which side of each frame will face out based on what looks best to you; for instance, if the legs bend, you may want to avoid having them turn inwards. Mark out holes for the upper rungs by measuring 19mm (¾in) down from the centre of the first upper tenon and marking a cross; for the lower rungs, measure 76mm (3in) down from the first lower tenon. Then repeat steps 14–20 to fix the remaining rungs into the legs.

Measure carefully *to ensure consistent spacing*

CONTINUED ☞

21 Weave the warp

Clamp the stool frame and tie the first tube to the corner of an upper side rung with a simple double knot. Bring the tube down and under the opposite rung, then up around and back to the starting point. Cover up the knot, and continue winding round in this way until you reach the opposite corner; the warp should be fairly tight.

Join one tube *to the next on the underside of the seat, with a sheet bend knot*

22 Weave the weft

To cross over from warp to weft, thread the inner tube under the adjacent rung at the corner, then bring it around and start weaving in and out of the warp, following the repeating pattern above right. You can make the weft very tight, to give strength to the seat. When you reach the diagonally opposite corner, fold the end of the last inner tube underneath the seat. Weave the tube in and out of the warp under the seat to provide friction, then tie it off with a double knot halfway down the underside of the weft.

Form the pattern by weaving with the weft tubes, here shown horizontally.

Line 1 – Lift over two and thread under two, repeating to the end.

Line 2 – Lift over one tube, then proceed as for line 1, threading under and over two tubes.

Line 3 – Start by threading under two tubes.

Line 4 – Start by threading under one tube.

The pattern
*works best with an
odd number of
rows to the warp*

After the fourth
*weft line the
pattern repeats*

23 Even out the legs

To finish off the stool, saw off around 25mm (1in) from the top of each of the legs. Then use a knife in thumb pull grip to shave the top of the sawn surfaces and chamfer the edges, creating a neat finish. Check the stool is level, and remove wood from the bottoms of the legs as necessary, making them all the same length.

**Technique: Levelling legs
– see p154**

Remove any protruding
*tenon ends
using thumb
pivot grip*

Design variations

The seat can be woven from other materials, such as wych elm bast or hickory bark for an organic feel. If you are using bark for the seat, weaker straight tenons could be used to join the components, since the frame would be under less torque. By adjusting the proportions of the frame, you can construct a table, or add height and multiple rungs to make a shelving unit.

TABLE

**Fit a solid
wood** *top,
planed flat*

Lengthen rungs
and shorten legs

CHAPTER 03

TURNING

Introduce turning wood on a pole lathe to your growing repertoire of skills, as your wood craft journey culminates in the sculpting and construction of a beautiful chair.

MAKE A
KITCHEN MASHER

This simple kitchen utensil works far better than the more usual perforated type of masher, and making it is a great way to trial and hone your turning skills. Once you have mastered planing cuts and rolling a bead, you will be ready to turn the spindles, posts, and legs of the Captain's Chair project that follows.

YOU WILL NEED

TOOLS & EQUIPMENT

- Pole lathe (*see pp224–45*)
- 4mm (⅛in) gimlet
- Oil
- Roughing out gouge
- Square chisel
- Spindle gouge
- Skew chisel
- Pencil and ruler

- Pull saw
- Spoon knife
- Straight knife

MATERIALS

- Cylindrical billet of green wood, around 325mm (12¹³⁄₁₆in) in length and 80mm (3⅛in) in diameter

SKILLS

YOU WILL LEARN TO

- Fit a billet to a lathe: *steps 1–2*
- Turn to size: *steps 3–4*
- Square ends: *step 5*
- Shape on the lathe: *steps 6, 10*
- Turn a bead, ball, and cove: *steps 7–9*

REMIND YOURSELF HOW TO

- Use a pull saw: *p24*

KNIFE GRIPS

- Thumb pull: *p21*

DESIGN GUIDE

Girth is retained at the masher end to give weight and surface area for the mashing action, and the tapered body gives greater access to corners of pans. The ball and bead offer gripping points, as well as decoration.

325mm (12¹³⁄₁₆in), inc. end waste

65mm (2⁹⁄₁₆in)

80mm (3⅛in)

BILLET VIEW

Concave *in the base improves mashing and allows it to stand upright*

Top decoration *consists of bead, cove, and ball*

66 THIS **TRADITIONAL** STYLE OF MASHER **DATES FROM** AT LEAST AS FAR BACK AS THE **18TH CENTURY.99**

> **LIFT** THE **CHISEL** OFF THE **WOOD** WHEN YOU **LIFT** YOUR **FOOT** OFF THE **TREADLE.**

TIP

Punching the centres with a gimlet helps the billet spin freely on the lathe without flying off.

The Process

1 Centre the billet

Start by placing your billet on to the centres of the pole lathe. Judge by eye where to position them, and aim to find the midpoint of the whole cylinder overall, not just the ends. Squeeze the ends just enough to hold it in place, then spin it all the way round to see if the position needs adjusting in any direction. If the cylinder is centred correctly it should run parallel with the tool rest. If one side is off then it can be gently tapped at the end to centre.

2 Punch and oil end holes

Crank the handle to push in the centres, then take the billet off the lathe. Use a 4mm (⅛in) gimlet to deepen the marks made by the centres. Twist the gimlet into the wood until you can no longer see the lead screw, then pull out. Insert a drop of oil in each hole, to reduce friction. Then place the billet behind the string, wrap the string around it twice, and position the billet securely on the centres. If the string is wrapped around correctly the billet will spin down towards the tool rest.

1. Without spinning, take a thin shaving with the tool on the rest to get an idea how to angle it; remember to have the bevel rubbing.

2. Avoid catching the trailing tip: a risk if you angle the chisel too low, as shown.

3. Use the tip to guide you: it is easiest to use the first third of the edge closest to the leading tip. Skimming a fine shaving with the very tip engaged gives great accuracy.

Wrap the string
around the opposite end of the billet to where you are cutting

3 Rough out the shape

Hold the roughing out gouge so the bevel rubs against the wood and raise the handle to engage the cutting edge. Move the gouge along, taking off shavings to create an even surface – go halfway across, then flip it round to do the other side. Look at the profile of the billet, rather than at the tool; take the peaks off then smooth into the round. When trying to get the bevel to rub on the raised, rather than lower, parts of the billet, do not push the bevel in as it will just move inwards to the lower parts. Instead, proceed the tool a small amount and hold it there as the wood spins; run a couple of passes like this before smoothing it in, edging bit by bit, roughing out a section at a time.

4 Create a smooth cylinder

. Switch to a square chisel taking off wider shavings for a smooth surface. Angle the blade to make cuts, skimming along with the tip of the chisel; try not to let the trailing end catch (see above). For a really straight cylinder, for a rolling pin, for example, you can rub a wax crayon on a straight edged bit of wood and hold it on to the billet as you turn.

CONTINUED ☞

The method is essentially the same for cutting the square end to a piece and the V-notch of a bead. Both are made by rubbing only the edge of the bevel against the wood, and all cutting is done with the tip of the blade edge. To square the end, hold the corner of the bevel square on; for a V-notch, tilt the chisel so that the bevel is at the desired angle.

Majority of bevel does not rub on wood

Rub the bevel only at the shaded corner

Square to the centre by lifting handle and moving in with the tip

RUBBING EDGE OF BEVEL

SQUARING OFF

Leave about 20mm (¾in) of wood around the centre

5 Square the ends
To square an end with the spindle gouge, first create a little shoulder, going in straight with the flute vertical and the bevel rubbing underneath. Then turn the gouge on its side to cut across the end towards the centre, resting the bevel on the shoulder. Take care not to damage the gouge by hitting the centres. For a flatter, smoother finish, switch to a skew chisel to finish off the end.

6 Remove waste from the handle end
Move the string to what will be the masher end. The handle should constitute around two-thirds of the total length of the masher. Begin building up a concave cut to form the neck. In the centre of the valley you are creating, hold the tool straight, and on the sides, angle the tool towards the centre. When you are happy with the thickness at the masher end, remove material from the rest of the handle, keeping the top section relatively flat.

SHAPING A BALL AND BEAD

Lift the handle and roll the chisel, pivoting your hand on the tool rest. The more skewed the cut, the sooner you come out of the lift-and-roll and the smoother the curve. Once the skew edge is vertical any more rolling may cause the corner to catch. Instead, bring the handle around by pivoting the bevel on the bead, and slide the body of the chisel along the tool rest.

Start the action *with the chisel square on*

This action *cuts two-thirds of the bead*

Lift handle *and move it to the right*

Use the bead *as the pivot point for the bevel*

SQUARE START   LIFT-AND-ROLL   BEAD PIVOT

7 Begin the decoration

Move the string to around the neck of the masher and shift your attention to decorating the top end. Decide on the widths of the ball, cove, and bead, then measure and draw pencil guidelines on the billet, allowing for waste next to the centres. Score straight in over the pencil lines with the tip of the skew, maintaining an even pressure. Start off lightly, and once you are happy with the placement of each groove, push further in.

Spin faster *for a smoother finish on the decoration*

8 Round the ball and bead

Begin shaping the ball at the top of the handle by making a V-notch with the toe of the skew. Do not to let the edge of the skew catch. Work on either end of the ball in turn to create the steepest parts of the curve – the most difficult sections of the ball. Then work your way from the middle, using the heel in a rolling cut, to create a smooth sphere. Use the same technique to make the tighter radius for the bead; *see* above.

CONTINUED ☞

TIP

As you work you will find the centres wear in, so tighten the billet accordingly from time to time. If they squeak, add more oil.

Make the widest *part of the handle about one-third of the way down*

Hold the skew *sideways to shape between curves*

10 Tidy the handle

Move the string back to the end of the masher while you refine the handle; having the string placed at the widest part of the masher means it will turn slower, and greater rotation speed helps effect smoother cuts, so treadle extra fast to make up for it. Use the skew for fiddly sections, and the square chisel for gentle slopes, to blend the shape of the handle into an even curve. First cut a convex, working to the edge of the bead on one side, then work down the gradual slope of the handle, blending it into the concave section. Keep your top hand loose enough to let the chisel slide, and delicately push the bevel onto the wood.

9 Make the cove

Continue working with the skew to make a triangular peak between the two grooves that border the cove section; this leaves neat shoulders either side of the cove and is far easier to do prior to gouge work. Switch to the spindle gouge to take off the peak of the triangle and cut a cove. Be careful not to remove too much here; if you do go too far with the spindle gouge, it is difficult to re-shape on either side with the skew.

Aim for a *shallow but defined depression*

> **" UNLIKE A GOUGE, A SKEW CHISEL WILL OFTEN NEED TO BE SHARPENED AS YOU WORK. "**

Design variations

Make a juicer or pestle for a mortar by carving a bulbous end on a smaller billet. The juicer grooves are started by drawing evenly spaced radius lines at the bulbous end, from which the straight lines can be marked with dividers.

JUICER

Carve wide grooves *using a knife, V-gouge, or saw*

PESTLE

The handle *should fit snugly in a clenched fist*

Make the crushing *end wide and flat*

Draw the knife *towards you, rotating the masher*

11 Add a V-cut

These are added for aesthetic interest at the point where a convex blends into a concave; they draw the eye in and distract from any imperfections in the transition. Go in straight with the toe, then square up and neaten the edge created with the heel, coming back from the handle end. Then put the string back into the neck and, with the square chisel, smooth the convex into the notch.

12 Trim the ends

Remove a little more of the waste beyond the ball. Take the masher out, and saw off the protruding ends with a pull saw. Use a spoon knife in thumb pull grip to carve off the last of the waste at the masher end; because we turned this end slightly concave, a straight knife would leave a little knobby bit. Trim the waste at the ball end with a straight knife, also in thumb pull grip.

MAKE A
Captain's Chair

Crafting a chair draws upon all the skills and techniques learnt by working through all the projects in this book. If you are confident in your abilities, this beautiful chair should mark the satisfying culmination of your mini apprenticeship. The design is based on a traditional captain's style, but without the need for steam bending of the arms and crest.

You will need

TOOLS & EQUIPMENT

- Pencil and measuring equipment, including metal ruler and pair of compasses
- Axe and axeblock
- Draw knife and shaving horse; *see p214*
- Electric drill with drill bits and reamer attachment
- Straight knife
- Pole lathe; *see p224*
- Roughing gouge
- Square and skew turning chisels
- Vernier or caliper gauge
- Tenon cutter
- Mortise block
- Auger
- Tape (for marking depth on auger and drill bits)
- Bowl gouge(s)
- Scorp
- Frame saw
- Bench hook
- Swizzle sticks
- Clamps

MATERIALS

- Tracing paper and pricking pin for templates
- PVA glue
- For the crest: 1 straight-sided billet of green wood, a little larger than the sizes indicated on the templates; this could also be sawn from dry wood
- For the turned elements: 14 x green wood cleft billets; split the legs and stretchers first as any fails in these will probably work out for posts
- For the seat: section of plank 51mm (2in) thick, planed flat and parallel; *see p100*
- For the arms: 2 x straight-sided billets of green or dry wood, a little larger than the sizes indicated on the template
- For wedges and pegs: billets of wood in contrasting hues
- Offcuts for block and wedges to size the legs

Skills

YOU WILL LEARN TO

- Use tracing paper templates: *steps 1, 17*
- Make and use a mortise block: *step 16*
- Use a scorp: *step 24*

REMIND YOURSELF HOW TO

- Shape with an axe: *p50*
- Use a draw knife: *p94*
- Use an electric drill: *p24*
- Carve a chamfered edge: *p16*
- Fit a billet to a lathe: *p146*
- Turn to size on a lathe: *p146*
- Use a tenon cutter: *p130*
- Turn a bead on a lathe: *p146*
- Drill angled holes: *p56*
- Use a reamer: *p130*
- Use a bowl gouge: *p82*
- Form a tenon and mortise joint with wedge: *p108*
- Peg joints: *p130*

> 66 MAKE SURE YOU HAVE **HONED** YOUR **TURNING** **SKILLS** BEFORE EMBARKING ON THIS PROJECT. 99

DESIGN GUIDE

Use these diagrams to guide you as you shape the components of your chair. All the turned pieces – the legs, the spindles, the arm posts, and the stretchers – are made whilst the wood is still green, and then left to dry, and shrink, before being finished. This shrinkage should always be taken into account when measuring; follow the dimensions in the diagrams below.

The scale templates for the arms, seat, crest base, and crest can be photocopied at 326 per cent. The dotted lines on the seat template diagram represent sightlines – you should sight down these lines when drilling the holes for the armposts and spindles. The angles indicated on the seat template are the angles at which the mortises should be drilled.

502mm (19¾in)

444.5mm (17½in)

222mm (8¾in)

57mm (2¼in)

9.5mm (⅜in) ø

44.5mm (1¾in) ø

28.5mm (1⅛in) ø

28.5mm (1⅛in) ø, 33mm (1⅝in) ø when green

LEGS

89mm (3½in)

133mm (5¼in)

324mm (12¾in)

216mm (8½in)

50.8mm (5⅞in)

57mm (2¼in)

16mm (⅝in) ø, 19mm (¾in) ø when green

15mm (⁹⁄₁₆in) ø

12.7mm (½in)

35mm (1⅜in) ø

26mm (1in) ø, 30mm (1³⁄₁₆in) ø when green

CREST AND ARM POSTS

483mm (19in)

16mm (⅝in) ø, 19mm (¾in) ø when green

16mm (⅝in) ø, 19mm (¾in) ø when green

25.4mm (1in)

38mm (1½in) ø

25.4mm (1in)

CENTRE STRECHER

381mm (15in)

16mm (⅝in) ø, 19mm (¾in) ø when green

16mm (⅝in) ø, 19mm (¾in) ø when green

25.4mm (1in)

38mm (1½in) ø

25.4mm (1in)

SIDE STRECHER

322mm (12¹¹⁄₁₆in)

235mm (9¼in)

20.5mm (¹³⁄₁₆in) ø, 24mm (¹⁵⁄₁₆in) ø when green

11mm (⁷⁄₁₆in) ø, 12.7mm (½in) ø when green

14mm (⁹⁄₁₆in) ø

30mm (1³⁄₁₆in)

SPINDLES

28.5mm (1⅛in) ø

57mm (2¼in)

Arm post *hole*

395mm (15⁹⁄₁₆in)

80mm (3⅛in)

30mm (1³⁄₁₆in)

40mm (1⁹⁄₁₆in)

40mm (1⁹⁄₁₆in)

Crest post *hole*

ARM TEMPLATE

30mm (1³⁄₁₆in)   30mm (1³⁄₁₆in)   30mm (1³⁄₁₆in)   30mm (1³⁄₁₆in)   30mm (1³⁄₁₆in)

85mm (3³⁄₈in)

175mm (6⁷⁄₈in) from seat front

20°   20°

100mm (3¹⁵⁄₁₆in)   100mm (3¹⁵⁄₁₆in)

100mm (3¹⁵⁄₁₆in)   14°   120mm (4³⁄₄in) from seat front   14°   100mm (3¹⁵⁄₁₆in)

32mm (1¼in)   32mm (1¼in)

14°   38mm (1½in)   85mm (3³⁄₈in)   85mm (3³⁄₈in)   38mm (1½in)   14°

SEAT TEMPLATE

365mm (14³⁄₈in)

76mm (2in)

Positions *of mortises*

CREST BASE TEMPLATE

365mm (14³⁄₈in)

112mm (4⁷⁄₁₆in)

10mm (³⁄₈in)   20mm (¹³⁄₁₆in)   25mm (1in)   20mm (¹³⁄₁₆in)   10mm (³⁄₈in)

Positions *of pegs*

CREST TEMPLATE

TIP

If it's hard to work the centre of the crest with a draw knife, try carving across the grain with a gouge to avoid tearing in.

The Process

1 Mark the crest outline

Use the template to transfer the curved shape of the crest and centre points of the spindle and post mortise holes to the base of the crest billet. Mark by pricking holes through tracing paper into the wood and joining up the dots to form a pencil guideline. Mark the outline on the top of the billet, too, but not the mortise holes.

2 Shape the curving body

Rough shape to the guidelines with an axe, starting in the middle and working back out to the edge. When forming the curves, remember the grain direction changes at the deepest point of the curve and needs to be worked to or from the centre. For safety when axing the parts closest to the ends, lay the crest on the block and use the edge of the block as a stop: aim the axe to carve and then follow through into the edge of the block.

Technique: Shaping with an axe – see p50

Give plenty of clearance *so there is no risk of the lead screw protruding*

Shape a gentle curve *to the top of the lumbar area, between the scallops*

3 Drill mortises and set the side scallops

Refine the basic shaping with a draw knife on a shaving horse. While the crest is still easy to clamp, drill holes 30mm (1³⁄₁₆in) deep at the mortise points on the base, marking with tape the depth on the drill bit. (When the crest has dried, you may need to redrill with the same bit if they have closed up a little in shrinking.) Now hold the bit against the front of the crest and aligned with a post mortise. Mark a line to indicate the depth of the mortise and another line higher up, well clear of the bit. Repeat at the other end, then draw out the scalloped sides of the crest so that they come in just above the clearance lines.

Technique: Using a draw knife, using an electric drill – see pp94, 24

4 Finish shaping the crest

Chop out the scalloped sides with an axe. To give lumbar support, the front of the crest rises up straight initially, before tilting backwards by 9–10° from where the side curves begin. Work this profile into the main body of the crest, then go over the crest again with a draw knife to finesse shaping and smooth the surface. Refine further and chamfer all edges with a straight knife. Leave the crest to dry for about seven weeks; the first week should be gentle, then it could be placed near a radiator or in an airing cupboard.

Technique: Carving a chamfered edge – see p16

CONTINUED ☞

> **"TENON CUTTERS** MAKE LIFE **EASY.** WITH **PRACTICE** YOU CAN **LEARN** TO TAPER **ENTIRELY** ON THE **LATHE."**

5 Size a spindle cylinder

Centre and fit a spindle billet to the lathe. Start turning with a roughing gouge, taking it down in size and shaping it to a cylinder of the maximum diameter. To judge the size, taper one end thinner than the maximum diameter, then set a vernier or caliper gauge to the maximum diameter and slide it along from the thin end until it catches. Mark that point with a pencil line and turn the rest of the cylinder until it is level with this guide, switching to a large square chisel to take off wider shavings for a smooth finish. Before you begin turning the tenons, note that you turn them wider when green to allow for shrinkage and that the initial taper is short. Tenons are re-turned when dry with a longer taper but at the same gradient. It is critical that the full length of the taper is flat and at the correct length and angle.

Techniques: Fitting a billet to a lathe, turning to size – see p146

6 Turn the seat tenon

The tenons are turned longer than needed to 57mm (2¼in), for some leeway. Ensure you are accurate with the size of the taper and with the location of the widest point of the tenon on the spindle. Turn solely on the lathe, or use a tenon cutter as well. Taper to the tenon on the lathe, blending the convex of the spindle bulge into the tenon, which needs to have a flat surface. Remove enough material to fit the tenon cutter.

Technique: Turning a taper – see p146

TIP

Green wood turned so thin can fly off. Use sharp tools and set the string close to the metal centre on the fatter side, to avoid.

7 Switch to a tenon cutter
Remove the spindle from the lathe and give it a few twists in the tenon cutter, taking care to keep the spindle centred in the cutter. The benefit of using the cutter is to help set a correct angle to the taper. Remount the spindle on the lathe and finish turning the tenon, copying with your chisel the angle set by the cutter. Use a caliper set to the right diameter and be certain you maintain the maximum diameter at the correct location on the spindle.

Technique: Using a tenon cutter – see p130

A "shoulder" left by the cutter indicates the extra material to remove on the lathe

8 Turn the crest tenon
Turn to size the other half of the spindle. The tenon into the crest is straight rather than tapering. The width is set halfway along the spindle, tapering down from the fattest point to give a long straight run in to the crest mortise. Leave the end 10mm (³⁄₈in) oversized so that the centre marks from the lathe can be sawn off. Turning green wood so thin can be tricky (*see* Tip, above) and you may find it easier when dry; if so, leave the crest tenon end thick and finish turning once the spindle has dried.

CONTINUED ☛

> ❝ REMEMBER THAT MOST TENONS NEED TO BE LEFT WIDER AND WITH A SHORTER TAPER TO ACCOUNT FOR SHRINKAGE. ❞

9 Finish the non-beaded components and start on a leg

Follow the same process in steps 5 to 8 to turn the other spindles and the symmetrically tapered stretchers. Now select a leg billet and turn it to a cylinder of the correct maximum diameter. Mark a pencil line at 95mm (3¾in) for the start of the bead decoration and then 12mm (½in) apart for each of the four V-notches for the beads.

Technique: Turning a bead – see p146

10 Set up the beads and taper the end

Score straight grooves at the pencil lines for the bead with the tip of a skew chisel. Switching to the square chisel, taper the end to a shallow concave with the correct diameter and final finish. This part can now be used for the string and since it is a thinner diameter the wood will spin faster and give better results for the beads. Set up the beads by cutting four V-notches at the grooves.

TIP

For good control, keep the tool rest close to the turning piece and lift off the chisel when you lift your foot from the treadle.

Keep the maxium
diameter 44.5mm (1¾in)

Rest the bevel
against the wood surface to help angle the cut

11 Shape the leg beads

Shape the curved sides of the beads. Take your time to get your body position correct and think where you need to end up at the end of each cut. It is usually helpful to round the same side of each of the three beads before switching your body around and doing the other side of the same three. Score a line at the point of greatest diameter, which is where the stretcher tenon will be fitted.

12 Turn the rest of the leg

Curve a taper from the scoreline, but without touching it, back towards the beads. Be very careful for the last 2mm (¹⁄₁₆in) before reaching the top bead so as to not damage it. At the other end, take the last third of the leg down close to the maximum green diameter of the tenon. Gently curve a convex taper from the scoreline, again without touching it, towards the tenon end, to blend with the previous cuts. Mark the widest point of the tenon measured from the score line and taper to the correct dimensions. Repeat steps 10 to 12 to turn the other three legs.

CONTINUED ☞

TIP
Keep the turned pieces somewhere warm and dry, such as an airing cupboard, so that they shrink fully before being fitted.

13 Size and mark up an arm post

With a roughing gouge and then square chisel, turn an arm post billet to a perfect cylinder 35mm (1⅜in) in diameter. Measure and mark the tapered tenon, then measure up from the top of the tapered tenon to mark the top of the bead. Mark another line 12.7mm (½in) back for the base of the bead.

14 Turn the arm post bead

Switching to the skew chisel, use the tip to cut straight grooves at the bead lines. Set up the beads by cutting V-notches at the grooves. Round the sides of bead as described in step 11.

Turn the tenon *until no high points are indicated*

15 Finish shaping the arm post

Taper the main body of the post down to the base of the bead. Beyond the top of the bead, turn the cylinder down to a diameter of 19mm (¾in) to form a straight tenon for the arm mortise, allowing for shrinkage. Repeat steps 13 to 15 to form the second arm post and the two crest posts. Leave all the turned pieces to dry for one to two weeks. Check the diameter of pieces regularly to verify when they have finished drying, allowing for 10 per cent tangential shrinkage. Alternatively, weigh the components regularly and once their weight is steady for a few days, you will know they are dry.

16 Re-turn the dried pieces

After drying, check the diameters of each tenon and re-turn them to the correct size. Mortise blocks are a good way to fine tune tenons. Make them by reaming the correct mortise in an offcut, then saw the block accurately in half. Cover the inside of the mortise with pencil lead, then give it a few turns around the tenon. Any high points will be revealed by pencil marks, which you can use as a guide for where to remove more material. Once the tenon matches the block you will get a solid block of graphite on the tenon.

Techniques: Squaring the ends, reaming holes with a drill – see pp146, 130

CONTINUED ☞

TIP
An auger drill bit with
an extender is helpful, as
the extra length amplifies
your ability to sight
angles accurately.

17 Mark up the seat

Transfer the seat template to tracing paper
and mark on to the pre-planed plank the
outline of the seat and guidelines for the post
and spindle decks. Mark crosses to indicate the
position of each mortise hole, and also draw on
any sightlines; it is along these lines that you
set the angle for drilling and reaming angled
mortises. The sightlines for the legs will need to
be re-drawn on to the underside for reaming; they
are drilled from the top, reamed from the bottom.

18 Drill leg holes

Drill a leg mortise hole to the
correct width and angle. Set the
angle with a sliding bevel and try square,
measuring from 90° upright. Through its
height, the try square shows the plane of
the sightline; align the bevel within this
plane and lean the drill back accordingly.
Mark with tape the drilling depth, which
matches the tenon length. Ideally, get
someone to help sight the angle as you
drill. Drill all seat holes in the same way,
following any angles and sightlines.

Technique: Drilling angled holes –
see p56

Line up the extender *with the scoreline of the other leg*

A manual brace *gives greater control as it allows you to ream more slowly*

20 Drill stretcher holes

Ream and dry fit the other legs. As you fit each leg, mark a number or letter on the corresponding leg and hole to avoid any mix-ups at the final fit. Mark points for drilling the mortise holes on the scored stretcher lines of one pair of front and back legs. The growth rings in the stretchers should be 90° degrees to the grain direction in the component with the mortise, so the tenons don't split the mortises with changes in humidity. Wrap tape on the drill bit to the correct mortise depth. Since you cannot drill straight across, to avoid drilling at an angle and missing the diameter line, twist the leg so that it is around 2mm (¹⁄₁₆in) offset, or whatever makes the mortise centred on the stretcher. Position the bit on the mortise mark and carefully line it up level with both stretcher score lines, then drill. Turn around and repeat on the opposite leg, then drill stretcher mortises on the other pair of legs.

19 Ream leg holes

Fit a reamer for the leg holes to a brace or electric drill. Mark the reaming depth on the side of the bit with a pen. Ream the hole to the same angle it was drilled at, and sight as for drilling. Test the fit by first measuring the distance from the seat to the scoreline, aiming for 222mm (8¾in). This is where the stretchers will be fitted and also acts as a fixed point for verifying the fit. Insert the leg and measure from the scored line with a divider; if it falls short, measure how much and ream to this depth. Test several times and get it right.

Technique: Using a reamer – see p130

CONTINUED ☞

> **TIP**
> Measure the mortise depth and distance between the legs from the same point, to take account of the curved surface of the stretcher.

Measure from *the outermost edge of the mortise rims*

21 Check lengths and re-turn

Work out the final lengths of the stretchers by measuring the distance between the mortise holes, then adding on the mortise depths. Transfer to the stretchers, always measuring from the centre points. Re-turn the stretchers to size, making square cuts with the skew on the stretcher side, and angled-in V-cuts on the waste side; a small chamfer on the tenon can also help when fitting. Saw off the waste end and tidy with a knife.

22 Drill holes for the middle stretcher

Dry fit the side stretchers, twisting them so that their growth rings are 90° to those of the legs; this is the grain orientation so that the most movement caused by humidity changes will occur along the length of the leg and not across it, which risks splitting. Mark a centrally positioned drill hole at the midpoint of the bulge on each stretcher. Wrap tape on the bit to the mortise depth. Again, since you cannot drill straight across, to avoid drilling at an angle, twist the stretcher so that it is 2mm (¹⁄₁₆in) offset, before lining up the drill bit between the stretchers. Drill and repeat on the opposite side.

Grip the scorp with your arms tucked in so that the scraping action comes from your whole body.

Keep the action fast and follow the sequence of: start cut, follow through, then lift, unless you can see clearance behind.

Take care! As soon as you see the wood fibres starting to tear, change the direction of your cuts.

23 Mark the seat hollow

Draw freehand the shape of the hollow on to one side of the seat, including the buttock indent and the line of the "pommel", which is the central raised section towards the front of the seat that demarcates the thigh indents. Leave at least 6mm (⅜in) clearance from the spindle deck. To ensure symmetry, copy the lines on to tracing paper, then flip the paper and transfer to the other side. Drill two 18.5mm (¾in) depth holes to indicate how deep to carve the hollow, drilling either side of the centre line towards the rear of the buttock indent.

24 Excavate the hollow

Start carving out the buttock indent, using a bowl gouge and mallet to cut across the grain, always towards and only as far as the centre line; this step could also be done with an adze. Taper the indent up towards the pommel line, excavating until the depth holes no longer appear. Switch to a scorp – a tool with a wider radius than the gouge that leaves a fine finish – to smooth over the gouged surface of the indent and blend it in with the edge of the spindle deck and up to the pommel; *see* above. If you don't have a scorp, use a shallower bowl gouge instead, taking off fine shavings.

Technique: Using a bowl gouge – see p82

CONTINUED ☞

TIP
You can cut the chamfer by eye, or mark equidistant guidelines on the seat and side faces to ensure consistent width.

25 Excavate the thigh scallops

Cut out the front edge of the seat with a frame saw, then draw guidelines for the thigh scallops, which should come down to between a half and two-thirds of the depth of the seat, leaving the pommel in between them. Mark the centre of the seat and the edge of each arm deck, then mark the lowest point of each scallop midway between and freehand draw curved lines connecting the points. Hollow the scallops with a draw knife, skewing it to cut across the grain. Cut a steep bevel initially, to the full depth of the scallop at the front, then roll it back into the seat by taking off corners in a series of progressively wider and shallower cuts.

26 Finish the seat

Blend in the thigh scallops with the buttock indent, first with the draw knife and then scorp or bowl gouge for finer blending. Saw out the back and sides of the seat, then return to the draw knife to cut a thick chamfer along all the sharp edges, and refine the sawn surface across all faces.

Hold the draw knife *on the skew as you cut across grain*

Use a mallet *to firmly fit the legs into their mortises*

Keep checking *you are following the guideline*

Mark orientation *lines from legs to stretchers and between stretchers*

27 Saw slots in the legs and dry fit the undercarriage

Dry fit the legs and mark centre lines across the end; they should be at 90° to the grain direction in the seat (left to right) so that when the wedges are inserted they don't split the grain. Mark centre lines down the sides of each tenon to help saw straight. Saw slots down these lines to, at most, three-quarters of the tenon length; the joint wedges are inserted into these slots. Dry fit the legs with the stretchers to form the undercarriage. Mark leg numbers or letters on the side stretchers, and draw orientation lines running from the central stretcher to side stretchers, so that you can realign when gluing.

28 Glue and fit the undercarriage

Take the undercarriage apart and then glue it together in stages, starting with the two side panels and then joining them together with the central stretcher. Apply the glue to the surface of each mortise hole with a swizzle stick, working quickly before the glue sets and matching up numbers and orientation lines. When the stretchers are all glued, bang home the leg tenons: the sound of the whack goes up an octave when they are fully inserted.

CONTINUED ☞

MAKING WEDGES AND PEGS

Once the wood has been batoned to small blocks, pegs and wedges can be made easily with a large, flat chisel.

1 For wedges: Support the block on a bench hook upright. With both hands on the chisel, use your body weight to pare the block to a taper. The wedge should be a fraction wider than the end of tenon, with parallel sides to the thin end.

2 For the pegs: Using a 5mm (³⁄₁₆in) drill bit for sizing, pare the wood down to square sides, then remove the corners with a knife to form an octagon. Chamfer both ends to prevent the fibres from fluffing.

1.

2.

29 Wedge the leg tenons

Fashion four wedges for the leg joints; *see* above. Glue and knock the wedges into the sawn tenon slots. Apply glue to one side only of the wedges, as otherwise they can come loose when the slots expand due to atmospheric changes: glued on one side they will stay stuck to that side of the slot until it closes back up again. Tap in the wedge with the back of an axe, hammer, or small mallet.

Technique: Wedging a tenon and mortise joint – see p108

Wedges need *to be ever so slightly wider than the tenon*

30 Remove the wedge waste

Once the glue has dried, saw off most of the protruding waste and pare the rest with a bowl gouge. Take care to protect the seat surface when sawing. One option is to clamp a flexible metal ruler to the seat and against the wedge, and to use the ruler as a protective surface to saw against. When paring with the gouge you are cutting across end grain, so only cut to the middle and move around the tenon; once down level with the seat you can take a single cut right across.

TIP
If you need to make minute adjustments to the width of a tenon, take a fistful of sandpaper and twist it round.

31 Drill spindle peg holes

Now fit and peg the spindles. Mark centre lines from the spindle mortises down the back edge of the seat. Apply glue to a mortise and tap the spindle into place. At the midpoint of the centre line, drill a 5mm (³⁄₁₆in) hole, 45mm (1¾in) deep, straight down through the seat and the centre of the spindle. Repeat for the other spindles.

Technique: Pegging joints – see p130

Hold the spindle *and rest your arm on the seat to keep everything steady*

32 Insert the pegs and true

Put a dab of glue on a peg and tap it into the hole with the back of an axe, hammer, or small mallet. Tap until you hear the pitch change, which means it has hit the back of the hole. Saw off most of the waste and pare away the remnants with a chisel or draw knife. Repeat for the other spindles.

CONTINUED ☞

TIP
Mark the mortise
positions with crosses
and place the centre point
of the drill bit precisely
on the crossing point.

**Drill all
the way**
*through
the billet*

33 Draw out an arm

Mark the shape of the arm on a billet. At one end of the billet, and offset to one side, draw a circle with a radius 40mm (1⁹⁄₁₆in) for the hand rest. At the opposite end and on the opposite side, mark a width of 40mm (1⁹⁄₁₆in) and draw a straight line to one-third of the length of the billet. Join this straight line and parallel straight edge to the circumference of the circle with pleasing curves, making space for a person's body to sit comfortably and keeping the grain aligned for strength at the crest end. Dry fit the arm posts and measure between the centre of their tenons to work out the mortise hole positions. Mark these points, then drill a straight hole to the diameter of the arm post tenon through the centre of the hand rest.

34 Start shaping the arm

Shape the arm with an axe and refine with a draw knife. Since the arm posts lean at 14° but the crest posts are perpendicular to the deck, the base of the arm must be shaped on the diagonal to fit square to the crest post. Test fit the arm; you may need to take a shaving or two from under the arm post mortise to allow the arm to sit back on to the crest post. Mark a line level with the top of the bead, and shave the base side to this angle. Shave the top of the arm parallel to this new datum, and taper it to the correct dimensions so that the back is slightly thinner than the front, which enables the arm to pleasingly tilt back, and is thin enough so that the crest can fit on to all of the post and spindle tenons.

35 Drill the crest post mortise

Place the arm on its arm post and hold the back flat against the bead of the crest post. Measure across from the tenon and mark on centrally the position of the crest post hole. Drill the hole square.

36 Refine the arm

Finish shaping the arm by rounding the hand end and creating a nice curved facet. Accentuate the curves back towards the crest; this allows the hand end to be rounded all the way back into this facet, which then continues back down the arm. The arm will stick out behind the crest; it can be sawn reasonably flush, but you may prefer the rustic look of it sticking out and there should be some length behind the hole for strength. If making from green wood, leave the arms to dry for eight weeks, drying gently for the first week.

CONTINUED ☞

> FASHIONING **PEGS** FROM WOOD OF **CONTRASTING COLOUR** TURNS A **PRACTICAL** ELEMENT INTO A **DECORATIVE** FEATURE. "

37 Fit the arms

Saw notches for wedges into both tenons of the arm posts, but just the seat tenons of the crest posts. Apply glue to the arm post mortise holes and to the seat mortise of the crest post, then fit the posts, attach the arm, and knock in the posts with a mallet. Glue and tap a wedge into the handle tenon of each arm post. Saw off most of the underseat excess of the arm and crest post tenons, leaving them slightly proud. Glue and tap in the wedges, then remove the excess.

38 Fit the crest

Make sure the spindle tenons are roughly equal in length to go into the crest, and that they are not so long that they bottom out in the mortises. Fit the crest piece on to the spindles and posts, and peg the tenons as per steps 31 and 32. Position the pegs for the crest posts at 10mm (³⁄₈in) up from the base of the crest, 20mm (¹³⁄₁₆in) up for the two outer spindles, and 25mm (1in) up for the central spindle, to achieve a pleasing curve to the peg positions that echoes the overall curve of the crest.

Cut a pencil in half *so that it lies flush to the top of the block*

39 Measure the leg heights

The final job is to level the legs. Sit the chair on a completely flat surface. Place a ruler horizontally near the front of the seat and measure the height of each front leg with another ruler; if there is a discrepancy the legs will need to be shortened. For comfort, the chair has a 12mm (½in) tilt from the pommel to the spindle deck, achieved by cutting the back legs shorter than the front. Measure the height at the back of the chair to work out how much you need to lower the back legs.

40 Wedge the legs level and cut to size

Insert small pieces of wood, or coins, under the legs until they are all level. Measure the distance from the floor to the bottom of the shortest leg, and cut a wood block to this height. Use the block to draw guidelines round the three longer legs, bearing in mind the back legs need to sit shorter for the tilt. Saw off the excess and cut a chamfer around the base of each leg with a knife in thumb pull grip.

CHAPTER 04

TOOLS

Get to grips with the key tools you need to craft with confidence. Discover their features, uses, and safety points, as well as how to sharpen and care for them so that they perform well and last.

TOOLS FOR SHARPENING

Sharpening tends to be done with abrasives, particles of a hard material that are used to scratch away the metal of the tool. This is usually done in a way that creates or maintains a specific shape, with progressively finer abrasives being used in succession to polish the edge. A polished edge not only cuts better, but also stays sharper for longer. Abrasives come in many forms, including sheets, bench stones, and diamond-plated metal plates.

The Process

GRINDER

■ **For general re-sharpening** a watercooled bench grinder is preferable. The slower speed of this machine makes it easy to control, and the grindstone is cooled by water, which prevents overheating and removes debris.

■ **The hollow ground** profile created by a bench grinder is very beneficial for many sharpening tasks, particularly for tools that need short flat bevels, such as axes and knives.

FILES

■ **Files can also be useful** for rough shaping of axes if you don't have the luxury of a motorized grinder, and they are necessary for sharpening saws.

■ **Most modern saws** are not designed to be sharpened, but learning to sharpen a saw is nevertheless a useful skill.

■ **Files can also be used** to sharpen large augers – do not sharpen the outside of augers, though, as this changes the size of the hole they cut.

Use two files, *one triangular and one round; always use a round file on a concave surface*

TYPES OF BEVEL

1. Flat bevel The bevels on cutting tools often need to be ground and honed flat, in order to smoothly guide the edge into the cut.

2. Hollow bevel A hollow ground surface allows you to create a flat bevel more easily and quickly, and is very good at returning a convex bevel to flat. Hollow grinding should be the preferred way for axes and knives.

3. Micro bevel A micro bevel – which is another, much smaller bevel at a steeper angle from the main bevel – is very useful for removing burrs and preventing edge roll. Unlike that of a secondary bevel, the edge on a micro bevel is still able to sever the fibres before they are split by the primary bevels.

A micro bevel *is created by stropping*

ABRASIVE PAPER

■ **Use a dowel** wrapped with wet and dry abrasive paper to sharpen the blade of a spoon knife, and other curved blades.

■ **It can help to rest** the knife on a raised block – if you just rest it on the table, you may find it gets in the way of the dowel.

■ **Try to find the flat surface** by feel, and work away from the edge and all the way around. Reposition the blade so that it is supported where needed.

■ **Abrasive paper** can also be used for flattening, using float glass as the flat substrate to put the paper on.

Use a diamond lapping plate to flatten a waterstone: draw a wavy pencil line on the surface of the stone, then rub the lapping plate against it until the marks disappear

JAPANESE WATERSTONE

■ **Japanese waterstones** are very efficient at cutting. They come in a variety of rough or fine grades; the number given refers to the number of particles, 600 grit being much rougher than 2500 grit.

■ **What makes them special** is how soft they are, continually revealing fresh sharp particles as the stone wears down. These are hard ceramic particles with sharp corners; as the stone is used, the particles lose their effectiveness, but if the block wears down to reveal new untouched particles it will sharpen tools efficiently again.

■ **Rough stones remove** more metal, but even fine Japanese waterstones remove quite a lot, meaning you can work quickly.

■ **The pictured stone** should be lubricated with water as it is used, and some will need soaking beforehand.

CONTINUED ☞

TIP

Long whetstones make it easier to move the tool in a flat motion – this is harder to gauge with a small slipstone.

> ❝ REMOVE MATERIAL IN LAYERS PARALLEL TO THE BEVEL, MAINTAINING THE ANGLE AT THE POINT OF THE BLADE. ❞

Metal particles *taken off the tool will clog up the stone – clean them off with a simple pencil rubber*

BENCH STONES

■ **Bench stones are so called** because they are usually large and used while supported on a bench; they tend to be solid ceramic blocks. The pictured technique works particularly well with a diamond stone as they are light and easy to hold. Because everything is held steady on the bench and you are looking down on to the bevel, it is easy to line up and accurately position your abrasions.

■ **Rest both the gouge** and the stone on the bench and, sighting down the bevel, use your left hand to guide and push the bevel against the stone, whilst moving the stone back and forth with your right hand in a flat motion.

■ **Good quality diamond stones** remain flat and last for a long time. This is very useful for when the bevel of a tool needs to be flat or accurate, but the blade itself is an ungainly shape or size, such that moving the tool across a fixed stone leads to inaccuracies.

HONING GUIDE

■ **You can use a honing guide** when sharpening chisels and planes on a bench stone. This allows you more control, which is particularly useful where you need an accurate secondary bevel, or just a very accurate flat bevel.

■ **Honing guides also work well** with abrasive sheets that have been glued on to large flat surfaces – float glass is sometimes used, being particularly flat.

FEELING FOR A BURR

Once enough material has been removed, the abrasive will push a tiny "burr" over the edge blade that can be felt overhanging the other side of the blade. Feel for it gently with the tip of your finger, brushing off the bevel away from the blade edge so as not to cut yourself. While the burr will tell you that you have sharpened right to the edge, it does not necessarily mean you have created a flat bevel.

Never run a finger *along the blade edge*

Do not overwork *one side in your efforts to create a burr*

BURR FORMED AT BLADE TIP

ASYMMETRICAL GRIND

SMALL DIAMOND STONE

■ **To flatten off the hollow grind** on an axe head, use a felt tip marker to draw on the bevel, then hone with a small diamond stone. As the blade is flattened, parallel silver lines appear through the pen marks.

■ **Do this on the bench** to protect your fingers: place the axe with the blade set just in from edge of the bench, so your knuckles are against the side of the bench as you sharpen safely away from the cutting edge.

■ **Using the marker pen** is a useful technique as it lets you see what is happening. If the bevel is convex, for instance, a silver line will appear quickly in the middle of the inky bevel; to flatten a convex you work to expand the silver outwards until all of the pen is removed from the bevel.

SLIPSTONE

■ **Slipstones are small abrasive stones** with a curved edge used for sharpening the flutes of gouges. Unlike bench stones, they are held in the hand during use.

■ **They can also be used** on straight knives to sharpen a flat surface. Place your finger on the other side of the stone, above where the bevel is, to hold the stone flat on the bevel; this works well with a small diamond stone too.

STROP

■ **Stropping is the final finishing step** in sharpening. Stropping can and should be used on most tools for the final polish and as a technique to brighten an edge between sharpenings. Stropping tools, or strops, tend to be made of wood or leather; if you can't plane a board very flat then a man-made board can be used effectively.

■ **Apply honing compound** to the strop and leave it to dry a little; Tormek paste is a good option as it is non-waxy and can be cleaned easily. Drag the edge of the blade up and down the strop. Move it away from the edge, which would dig into the blade. You are aiming to push the bevel on to the wood firmly enough to hold it flat. Keep working both sides of the edge until it gets polished and any burr is removed, being careful not to round the edge.

■ **Leather strops** can lead to rounding the edge over, which is problematic for many tools that should have flat bevels.

UNDERSTANDING A
Straight Knife

Mastering a basic wood carving knife is the foundation of green woodworking. This Scandinavian-style Mora knife, with its laminated blade and utilitarian handle, is the steadfast companion of any wood crafter.

Laminated steel
makes the blade hardwearing

Symmetrical
handle means it can be used in all knife grips

Rivet or peen
holds the tang at the base

Metal ferrule
keeps together the wood fibres of the handle

FOCUS ON...
Fitting the Handle

As an individual at home, drilling stepped holes to house the varying shape of the knife tang can be difficult; a technique that works well is "burning in". Drill a small hole through the handle and heat up the tang, but do not heat the edge. With the blade clamped in position, tap the handle on to the hot tang, opening up the hole where necessary.

Metal tang
narrows in two stages

"Peen" the end
of the tang by hammering it to secure the washer

Edge *loses temper if heated much past 200°C (392°F)*

SIDE VIEW, SHOWING TANG

> ❝ THE "SCANDI" GRIND IS SYNONYMOUS WITH THE ART OF WHITTLING. ❞

Tapering bevel *shortens towards the tip*

FEATURES

■ **Laminated blade** The blade has hard steel in the centre to maintain the cutting edge for longer. Softer steel on the outside gives strength and makes it easier to sharpen.

■ **Fixed blade** Many hand knives feature folding blades, but a fixed blade is far more preferable as it gives the knife more reliable cutting action.

■ **No finger guard** The lack of a finger guard makes it easier to form grips and get in close to the blade in order to direct the cutting edge with your fingers.

USES

■ **Carving and finishing** Use for whittling and as a tool for finishing edges and surfaces of larger projects.

■ **Splitting** Can be used to split out billets from small logs and start splits before inserting wooden wedges.

■ **Chip carving** Chip out details for decoration with the tip, including letter and figure carving, or carve out small square holes.

Safety Tips

▸ **Keep the knife** in its sheath when not in use and never walk with the blade exposed.

▸ **Take regular breaks** to maintain concentration.

▸ **Practise knife grips** thoroughly without cutting at first. Make sure you know the "stops" that prevent the knife from carrying through, and how to keep safe should the tool slip, by ensuring no fingers are in the path of the cutting action.

HOW TO
SHARPEN

The bevel needs to be very flat on a straight knife. Resist the temptation to sharpen the edge only, which alters the blade geometry.

The Geometry

The bevel needs to be long enough to guide the edge on a flat planing cut, but short enough to make tight concave cuts. A long bevel will dig into a tight curve and have a weak edge.

The bevel *rides flat on the wood and guides the cutting edge*

Edge angle *around 25°, equating to 7mm (¼in) bevels on the Mora knife*

25°

7mm (¼in)

CROSS-SECTION OF BLADE

The Process

1 Flatten the bevels
Make sure the abrasive you are using is flat, and move the abrasive in a flat motion in relation to the knife, or vice versa. Remove equal amounts of material parallel to the bevel on either side. Lift the handle very slightly to maintain contact at the tip.

2 Hollow grind
Use a whetstone grinder to form a hollow grind, which makes creating a clean flat bevel much more achievable; the biggest problem for beginners is rounding over the bevel.

3 Polish by stropping
Stropping regularly is very useful, but it is important not to round over the edge: a wood or MDF strop is recommended, rather than leather, which has too much give and rounds the edge.

Spoon Knife & Scorp

Both these tools are designed to make concave cuts for carving a hollow. A spoon knife tends to be used on smaller pieces. More power can be put into a scorp as it is employed with both hands, like a draw knife.

RAY ILES

Longer handles
enable levering cuts to be made with both hands

Blade geometry
similar to spoon knife but tends to have much shallower radii

Scorp

Spoon knife

Safety Tips

Store both tools in protective sheaths when not in use and never walk with blades exposed.

A spoon knife is most commonly employed in thumb pull grip. When carving in this grip it is crucial that your thumb is not in line with the direction of cut: keep it carefully tucked behind the piece instead.

SCORP

■ **Uses** A scorp can be used to hollow large bowls and small shallow dishes. It is also an excellent tool for excavating the indentation of a chair seat.

■ **Efficiency** A scorp is a very efficient hollowing tool, since the blade takes very wide shavings over a large surface area.

■ **Skewing** Just like a draw knife, the scorp can be skewed to take a finer cut.

> " SPOON KNIVES CAN ALSO BE CALLED BENT KNIVES BUT ARE NOT CROOKED KNIVES. "

Blades come
in a variety of curves, from tight to shallow and open

Most blades
cut in different radii depending on the part used

Spoon Knife

■ **Using on spoons** As the name suggests, spoon knives are commonly used to take concave cuts in spoon carving. As well as the hollow of the bowl, they will also carve a nice concave on the back of the bowl's transition into the neck, or a thumb indentation on the top of the handle.

■ **Other uses** They can also be used to carve the hollow of a cup, add texture to a butter paddle, or refine the interior surface of a bowl. This style of spoon knife with a "question mark" shaped blade is the most adaptable, other more open curves can be useful for shallower cuts.

FOCUS ON...
FITTING THE KNIFE HANDLE

Some people use the shrinkage of green wood to eventually hold the blade in place. If the knife has a flat cross-section, the space either side in the handle hole can be filled with split pieces of dowel gently tapered, glued, and tapped into place.

Top of blade
should be centred on the handle

If the tang is round *drill a hole and fix with epoxy glue*

SIDE VIEW, SHOWING TANG

SHARPEN

Key to sharpening both a spoon knife and scorp is to create a convex blade shape so that the edge does not dig into concave surfaces.

The Geometry

For a clean cut around the inside of a concave, the outside surface must be correspondingly convex. It is easiest to create two or more bevels, which could then be rounded to give control over the shape.

Thinner steel
allows for a finer edge angle

Long bevel

Ground bevel
on back of blade

Secondary bevel

BLADE CROSS-SECTIONS

a A single long bevel causes the edge to dig into the wood.
b With two bevels, the secondary bevel guides the edge and the long bevel provides shoulders for for levering the edge out of the cut.
c Blades made with thinner steel require a wider cross-section for strength, and can have a bevel taken off the back.

The Process

1 Work the inside
Sharpen the inside of the blade using wet-and-dry abrasive paper wrapped around a wooden dowel. Saw a fine slot halfway down the dowel for the paper to catch in and wrap around.

2 Work the outside
Sharpen the outside of the blade using a flat board with wet-and-dry paper adhered to it. Or alternatively a diamond stone works well. Keep control over the bevel length and aim for parallel lines; start with a 6mm (¼in) bevel and a secondary bevel on the very edge.

UNDERSTANDING AN

AXE & ADZE

These kindred dual-action tools can be used with force to quickly chop out waste material, or employed more gently to take fairly precise shaping cuts. The rounded blade of a bowl adze makes it suitable for hollowing.

AXE

■ **Chopping cuts** These produce chips and are made at a roughly 30° angle to the surface, slicing through the fibres of the wood and splitting it along the grain.

■ **Shaving cuts** Slicing at a shallower angle engages the bevels to take shavings rather than chips.

■ **Accuracy** With an axe, it is the plane of the swing, adjusted by wrist and arm for accuracy, that defines where the cut occurs.

Good width *at the top end of the handle is useful for flicking cuts*

WOOD TOOLS

Axe

Rounded end *can be held loosely with hooked middle finger, to swing out of cuts*

FOCUS ON...

FITTING THE AXE HEAD

Fit an axe head by knocking a wedge into the top of the handle through the centre of the "eye". To fix a loose head, carefully hammer with a chisel to open up room for the thin end of a wedge, then knock it in to splay the handle so the wood fills the eye. Leave part of the wedge slightly proud for future adjustments. If the eye is an hourglass shape, you can knock the head down lower to compress the fibres for a better fit.

Head loosens *as wood fibres of handle compress*

Wedge pushes *out sides of handle*

BACK VIEW WITH WEDGE CROSS-SECTION

> " BOTH ANCIENT TOOLS ARE EXTREMELY EFFICIENT AT REMOVING MATERIAL. "

Adze

Adze

■ **Cutting action** Like the axe, an adze can be used in two modes: chopping and shaving. Unlike an axe, most adzes cannot be used to chop down trees or split wood.

■ **Hollowing** The type of small adze with a tight curve shown here is ideal for creating hollows, such as in spoons, bowls, and the seats of chairs.

■ **Accuracy** The adze is a far more accurate tool than an axe because the edge is a fixed length from the pivot point at the handle. Adjusting the pivot point by moving your wrist accurately dictates where the cut will occur.

▶ Safety Tips

- **Consider the direction** of swing in case you follow through: don't put your body in the way!

- **Consider hand placement** when holding the work piece and ensure your technique gives complete control. Beware the axe may bounce off the wood if the edge doesn't bite.

SHARPEN

The cutting edge of an axe is most versatile with two straight bevels. An adze often has a problematic secondary bevel to work on.

The Geometry

Some people advocate a convex bevel on an axe, since it helps direct the blade out of the cut. Flat, short bevels, however, are more suited to general carving as they allow straight, convex, and shallow concave cuts to be taken. With an adze, the main issue is dealing with the steep secondary bevel often left by manufacturers.

Edge angle *will increase*

AXE BLADE CROSS-SECTIONS

a Grind two flat 9mm (⅜in) bevels either side of the edge; these are best created with a hollow grind first.

b If two bevels cause the edge to roll or wear too quickly, maintain length on the side predominantly used to take cuts by removing material from the opposite side.

Aim to reduce *the bevel to a shallower angle*

ADZE BLADE DETAIL

The Process

Sharpening an axe
Reshaping can be done with files/angle grinders/grinding belts and dry stone bench grinders, but it is best if the axe is first hollow ground with a motorised whetstone, and the hollow then flattened with a diamond stone.

Grinding an adze
Grind the secondary bevel on the inside of an adze blade with a drum sander attachment on an electric drill.

UNDERSTANDING A
FROE & WEDGE

Cleaving wood is the process of splitting out billets from fresh logs without the use of power tools, and it is the essential starting point of all green wood craft. After an axe and mallet, a froe and wedge are the next essential tools, increasing your ability to control the split.

The edge
should never be sharp enough to cut fingers

Froe

> **ROUNDED EDGES** HELP A WEDGE TO **LAST LONGER**. TOO MANY **SHARP EDGES** WILL MAKE IT PRONE TO **SPLITTING.**

FOCUS ON...
FITTING THE HANDLE

The handle of the type of froe shown here is fed through a tapering eye. The flared base of the handle allows it to be knocked securely into the eye; the tapering eye compresses the fibres making it stronger. The handle suffers a lot of compression from being hit with a mallet, so it is best to use fast-growing wood, which tends to be strong; look for five growth rings per 25mm (1in).

Eye tapers
slightly to fit flared handle

FROE SIDE VIEW, SHOWING EYE

Wedge

Chamfer the
edges *to prevent
damage*

FROE

■ **Controlled splitting** Combined with a cleaving brake, a froe is extremely effective for controlling splits down longer, thinner pieces. Hold the piece in a brake and, with both hands on the froe blade, put tension on the side where the split should run, then lever the wood open with your elbow on the end of the froe handle.

■ **Splitting fat logs** A froe is much better suited than an axe to splitting short, wide logs, which with an axe would require laborious scoring to split.

WEDGE

■ **Chasing splits** When carved from a tough hardwood, wedges can be used by themselves to split softer pieces. More frequently, they are used with a knife, axe, or froe to hold open splits once started, so that the split may be chased down the log.

■ **Wood versus metal** A wooden wedge is usually a far better choice than a metal wedge, since you rarely want to hit metal on metal. For example, a wooden wedge can be hit with force by a metal sledgehammer, or placed next to an axe in a split without fear of damaging the axe.

■ **Power ratio** A thin wedge with a shallow gradient provides a greater power ratio than a thick wedge, although it must be driven in deeper to widen the split the same amount.

▼ **Safety Tips**

When hitting the froe with a mallet, take care not to catch the knuckles of your hand gripping the handle.

Keep fingers outside of the split in case the split closes. The closing action can have great force, particularly with bigger logs.

Start slowly when hitting a wedge, since they can fly out, especially if they are thick.

SHARPEN

A froe needs to be blunt enough to grip firmly along the edge without fear of cuts. You may, however, need to sharpen a secondhand froe.

The Geometry

A froe does not have a distinct bevel to its blade, but it does have a relatively flat surface that enables it to penetrate wood easily. A thin edge to the blade, especially on a small froe, will help to prevent splits travelling too far.

Flat surfaces
*also help with
levering*

Thin edge
*doesn't widen a
split too quickly*

FROE BLADE CROSS-SECTION

The Process

Reshaping a secondhand froe
You may find some "mushrooming" of the profile shape on a secondhand froe because the previous owner used a metal hammer on it. If this is the case, you can flatten it and thin back the edge using a file or angle grinder.

Tenon Cutter & Reamer

While tapered tenon joints can be formed with an axe or draw knife and a straight knife, the tools shown here are useful when speed and greater accuracy are required. A tenon cutter shaves the end of a component to a tapered cylinder, while the reamer drills the corresponding tapered mortise hole.

Reamer

■ **Drill or brace** The reamer attachment can be fitted to an electric drill or a manual brace. You can gain greater control if turning by hand with the brace.

■ **Gradient of taper** Reamers are available with shallower angles; this one is around 12°. A finer gradient is arguably preferable since there is less material to remove, however, such tenons are more likely to split the mortise if hit home too hard.

Blades run *down the entire length of the reamer body*

Mark the depth *to ream to with felt tip pen*

Reamer

“THE CUTTER AND REAMER ARE LIKE POSITIVE AND NEGATIVE IMAGES OF A TAPERED TENON JOINT.”

Screws for *adjustments to the blade*

Tenon cutter

Tenon cutter

■ **Cutter sizes** Tenon cutters come in different sizes, for cutting both tapered and straight tenons. Cutters with diameters of 9.5mm (⅜in) and 16mm (⅝in), both with the same taper, were used for the tapered tenons in this book, and these cover the full range of the reamer shown.

■ **Positioning centrally** Keep the cutter centred on the end of the component, with an even gap all around.

■ **Using with a vice** By securing to a workbench with a vice, you can use two hands to turn the component.

■ **Blade adjustments** Blade alignment can make a difference in how the tenons match the reamed hole. Adjust with an Allen key after doing a test joint.

■ **Shrinkage** To form a tapered tenon on green wood allow 15 per cent for shrinkage. Focus on the maximum diameter of the component, plus 15 per cent, then through trial and error discover how far along the length of the tenon the cutter needs to be applied. Once found, make it quickly repeatable with a mark on the tenon for the correct length that should be cut.

■ Safety Tips

Be extremely cautious when using the reamer in an electric drill, when long, sharp blades are exposed and rotating at great speed.

Keep fingers well away from the blades and make sure the compenents being worked on are secured.

SHARPEN

To maintain efficiency and accuracy, both the reamer and tenon cutter should be kept properly sharpened.

The Geometry

The cutting blade of a reamer has a simple geometry and to keep it sharp requires only maintaining the flatness of the bevel. To sharpen the tenon cutter blade, follow the same edge geometry as when sharpening a plane; *see* p201.

Sharpen down *this surface on both sides*

REAMER OVERHEAD VIEW

The Process

Sharpening the reamer
Use a small diamond stone evenly over all parts of the blade bevel until completely flat. Some people use a burnisher (a polished hard steel rod) to turn a small burr on to the edge of a reamer, but it works fine without.

Sharpening the tenon cutter
Flatten the back of the blade, then grind the same angle of bevel as for a plane iron. Hone the micro bevel on a diamond stone; a honing guide can be useful for this.

DRAW & PUSH KNIFE

Two-handled knives make it easy to put your full body strength into cuts, which makes for more efficient shaping. As the names suggest, a draw knife is used by drawing it towards you, and a push knife by pushing it away.

> **A DRAW KNIFE** SHAVES MORE **QUICKLY** THAN A STRAIGHT KNIFE, AND IS MORE **ACCURATE** THAN AN AXE.

Push knife

Draw knife

FOCUS ON...
DRAW KNIFE HANDLES

Different styles of draw knife work in different ways. With both, you'll find if they are used the "wrong" way up the edge will dig in too much. Draw knives with cranked handles tend to be used bevel up and those with straight handles work best with the bevel down.

BEVEL UP

BEVEL DOWN

PUSH KNIFE

■ **Riving** A push knife is handy for cleaving thin sections of wood because it can be pushed downwards like a froe. Use a block and push away from your body.

■ **Pivoting** Use your wrists to pivot around cuts by rolling the bevel over concave or convex facets.

DRAW KNIFE

■ **Hardware** Most effective on a shaving horse, a draw knife can also be used on wood held in a vice.

■ **Even wear** The centre of the long blade tends to get worn down more quickly. Use different parts of the blade for more even wear, and pay attention to any differences when sharpening.

■ **Bevel up or down** A draw knife with a cranked handle and the blade bevel up (*see left*) is better for carving flat surfaces, since there is a longer section of metal in contact with the wood. With the bevel down, you are able to cut concaves and both knives will cut straighter if the blade is skewed.

Safety Tips

Always hold these knives with two hands, both when making cuts and when carrying.

Keep the edge in a fixed position from your body by tucking in elbows and moving your body to effect the cut.

SHARPEN

When sharpening a cranked bevel-up draw knife, use a large diamond stone to flatten the large, flat side of the blade, and a smaller diamond stone for the short bevel.

The Geometry

The final edge angle of a draw knife should be around 30–35°, and that of a push knife should be 25°. Take care not to lose this geometry when sharpening the blades.

25°

Flat bevel
on both sides

Beveled only
on one side

30–35°

DRAW KNIFE

PUSH KNIFE

The Process

1 Flatten wide back of the draw knife
Use a large diamond stone to achieve a flat surface on the wide section of the blade.

2 Additional bevels
Grinding a secondary bevel or micro bevel on the bevel-up drawknife works well.

3 Hollow grind
Start with a hollow grind for both the push knife and the bevel-down draw knife. They benefit from nicely honed flat bevels started from a hollow grind.

UNDERSTANDING

GOUGES

A gouge is basically a chisel with a curved edge to the blade and often also a curved profile down its length. They are used in relief carving and for shaping hollows both on and off the lathe.

Spindle gouge

Roughing gouge

Bowl or bent gouge

SPINDLE GOUGE

■ **Profile** A spindle gouge has a straight profile along its length that enables it to be used for turning.

■ **Uses** Use to countersink drilled holes. In turning, spindle gouges are used to shape details, in particular coves. They are also useful for squaring ends, especially when there is a lot of material to remove.

ROUGHING GOUGE

■ **Profile** Like the spindle, a roughing gouge also has a straight profile along its length.

■ **Uses** Use in the initial stages of turning to remove bulk. Also useful for creating concave cuts.

BOWL OR BENT GOUGE

■ **Profile** A bowl gouge has a curved profile along its length so that it is capable of carving hollows.

■ **Uses** As the name suggest, a bowl gouge is used to carve out hollows, such as for bowls. Also useful for trimming the wedges used to hold legs on carved seats.

■ Safety Tips

Fit protective sheaths over the gouge blades when not in use. Storing them in a tool roll is also helpful.

When using never place your hand or body in front of the cutting edge.

FOCUS ON...

FITTING THE HANDLE

Gouges designed to be hit with a mallet often have a ferrule at the end of the handle to keep the fibres together. The best gouges tend be socketed with a shoulder-like bolster that prevents the tang splitting open the handle when the tool is struck.

Bolster transfers
splitting force to edge

Metal ferrule
protects end

Blade fitted
to handle by tapering tang

OVERHEAD VIEW, SHOWING TANG

SHARPEN

Each type of gouge has a different cutting edge geometry that needs to be shaped in contrasting ways to keep them sharp.

The Geometry

Hone flat the bevel of a roughing gouge. A fingernail profile that takes the bevel further down one side is best for a spindle gouge. This produces a large edge, which can be used for skewed cuts and also gives greater access to the tip for tight cuts. The bevel of a bowl gouge is the same as a spoon knife: a gradual convex from the edge; *see* p187.

Grind a flat *bevel to around 30°*

"Swept back wings" *enable more of the blade to be used*

ROUGHING GOUGE BLADE

SPINDLE GOUGE BLADE

The Process

Sharpening roughing and bowl gouges

Both gouges are best ground on the whetstone grinder then honed flat; the techniques described in the sharpening section with the tool and diamond stone flat on the bench, work very well. Flatten the cannel with a slipstone or abrasive paper around a dowel.

Sharpening a spindle gouge

Work a spindle gouge on a bench stone. This allows you to roll the gouge around on the stone to hit all parts, while sighting down the bevel.

CHISELS

Chisels are key tools for removing excess wood precisely and quickly. With the edge at right angles to the handle, cuts are effected by pushing in line with the handle. In joinery, the flat back of a chisel is the foundation of the joints holding our furniture and homes together.

SKEW

■ **Skewed angle** The edge of a skew chisel is angled rather than square.

■ **Relief carving and turning** The skewed end can get into nooks and crannies; for the same reason they are good for turning. Tools for turning are often of stronger steel, however, and relief carving tools could be dangerous on a lathe. Both types of tools rely on their bevels to guide cuts; usually those for relief carving have longer bevels for paring.

■ **Use both hands** With the piece of wood you are working on secured, you can have both hands on the chisel – this triangulates the movement, giving you greater control.

Skew chisel

Square chisel

Mortise chisel

narex
Made in Czech Republic

SQUARE CHISEL

■ **Versatile tool** Having such a wide flat blade, this chisel can be used to flatten surfaces and for paring, such as making wedges.

■ **Corners may be taken off** You may wish to file off the corners, because, when used in turning, they have a tendency to scratch the surface of the spindle when the chisel is lifted to take a clean cut with the bevel in contact with the wood.

MORTISE CHISEL

■ **Used for cutting mortises** The size of the chisel determines the width of the mortise.

■ **Deep blade** This allows the sides to rub against the inside edge of the mortise to guide a square cut.

■ **May need reinforcing** If the end of the chisel is being hit, it may need a metal ferrule and either a bolster or socket, to withstand heavy use.

▌ Safety Tips

 Can be very dangerous – put protective guards on the ends when not in use.

 Hold with both hands if not using a mallet; it can be helpful to place one hand at the end of the handle, against your body, and the other around the main body of the handle.

SHARPEN

With a mortise chisel, you are relying on the long flat back to guide the cut, and the bevels are usually there to generate a sharp edge.

The Geometry

A secondary bevel can be particularly useful on a mortise chisel, and makes sharpening easier. Skews and square chisels used for turning, as in this book, should be sharpened with a hollow grind, so the bevel can rest against the curve of the turned billet.

Secondary bevel / 35° / 30°

Hollow ground in the centre, polished at top and bottom

Remove corners to prevent them from rubbing

MORTISE CHISEL CROSS-SECTION · SKEW CHISEL OVERHEAD VIEW · SQUARE CHISEL OVERHEAD VIEW

The Process

1 Flatten the back of the blade
It is worth putting effort in to make the long section of the chisel, on the other side from the bevel, entirely flat; Japanese waterstones and diamond stones are the most effective ways of achieving this. Once flat, it will need very little work beyond removing the burr from honing the bevel.

2 Hone primary and secondary bevels
Use a honing guide to help you as you sharpen the secondary bevel. Because the secondary bevel is shorter, it will take less time to sharpen.

UNDERSTANDING
Planes

Planes are used to reduce the thickness of boards, eliminate uneven surfaces, and create a smooth finish. They are particularly useful for shaving flat and true surfaces from which to set a datum face and edge.

Wooden scrub plane

66 AS YOU **GLIDE** THE PLANE OVER THE WOOD, THE **ANGLED BLADE** SHAVES THE SURFACE TO A **UNIFORM** FINISH. 99

Unscrew *the lever cap to release the blade assembly*

Jack plane, overhead view

Hold the rear *handle with your dominant hand*

Push the plane *with both handles to guide it in a flat motion*

Jack plane, side view

The sole or base *is made from very durable hardwood*

SCRUB PLANE

■ **Cambered blade** The scrub plane has a cambered, or slightly convex, blade, which allows it to take very thick shavings. This is particularly useful when you need to quickly remove waste material in order to flatten a warped surface.

■ **Aggressive cutting** A scrub plane can take very aggressive cuts because it is thin and short; if it were very wide and long it would only be able to take off the very highest points.

■ **Hold the same direction** Coming at 90° to an already scrubbed board, you will only nibble at the peaks of the furrows; by maintaining cuts in the same direction, you can take full-length shavings all along the tip of each furrow.

■ **Cut across the grain** If the wood does not have a predictable straight grain, go across the grain with the plane; a diagonal direction is often most efficient.

■ **Accessing the blade** The blade is secured by tapping the wedge with a plane hammer. Loosen the wedge by firmly tapping the heal of the plane sole on the top of the work bench; support the iron and wedge so they do not fall out.

JACK PLANE

■ **Versatility** A jack plane is multi-purpose and useful for flattening a plank that has first been scrubbed.

■ **Low-angled cutting** This jack plane is a bevel-up, low-angled plane, which means the blade hits wood at an acute angle. It has the benefit of working well on end grain, which higher angled planes struggle with.

■ **Adjustable mouth** The mouth of this particular jack plane can be opened and closed. When narrowed, the mouth applies pressure in front of the shaving and so prevents fibres splitting ahead of the edge. Open up the mouth to take thicker shavings.

■ **Safety Tip**

Planes have sharp blades too: protect both the edge and yourself from damage, especially when sharpening.

SHARPEN

Plane irons at a steeper angle deal with difficult grain more easily. A low-angle plane will be better able to smooth difficult grain if given a steeper secondary bevel.

The Geometry

A plane iron benefits from having a secondary bevel ground into the tip of the blade. Blades at a steep angle take cleaner cuts. If struggling with a shallow-angled blade, grinding a 2° secondary bevel effectively transforms it into a "high angle" plane.

Steep angle *bends back shavings to avoid tear out*

2° micro bevel

25° main bevel

Form a steeper *secondary bevel to replicate benefits of a high-angle plane*

STEEP BLADE CROSS-SECTION

PLANE BLADE CROSS-SECTION

SHALLOW BLADE CROSS-SECTION

The Process

1 **Grind the primary bevel**
Remove the blade and grind it to the correct angle on a grinding wheel, or by hand on a coarse bench stone. Continuously move the blade while grinding.

2 **Maintain a flat polished surface**
Polish the back with Japanese waterstones. Ensure the abrasive is perfectly flat; avoid rounding the edge.

3 **Hone a secondary bevel**
Check for a burr evenly along the length of the edge, then remove the burr with finer abrasives. It can be helpful to gently radius the final distance towards the corners of the blade, to prevent the corners digging in.

UNDERSTANDING A

FRAME SAW

A frame saw allows you to use a small blade, which is very useful to reduce friction compared to the wide blade of a handsaw. Once the windlass has been tightened, the saw is very sturdy. The thin blade also enables the saw to cut curves, and can be used instead of a bandsaw.

Hooked ends
*keep the tension-
providing string
held in place*

66 WITH THE CORRECT **BLADE**
THE **FRAME SAW** REALLY
COMES INTO ITS OWN. 99

FOCUS ON...
TYPES OF BLADE

The more "teeth per inch" along a saw blade, the smoother the cut, as a rule. Blades with larger teeth are used to remove material fast, but may leave a rough sawn surface.

Large teeth
*with wide gaps
take out more
material*

LOW TPI

Small teeth
*with narrow
gaps leave a
smoother finish*

HIGH TPI

**Split pins with
washers** *hold an
old bandsaw
blade in place*

String, tightly twisted, *provides tension*

Cross piece *gives the saw its strength*

Spanish windlass *allows you to tighten and untighten the string as needed*

Long handle *helps steer when rip sawing*

USES

■ **Replacement for a bandsaw** Despite its somewhat delicate appearance, a frame saw with the correct blade can cut curves through thick pieces of wood.

■ **Cutting curves** Blade rotation allows for curved cuts. Use smaller versions or fretsaws/coping saws for delicate work, such as removing waste from dovetails.

■ **Interior cuts** The blade can be detached and inserted through a drilled hole, to make interior cuts.

Safety Tips

Check the saw is in good condition before use. Make sure the string is intact; it is advisable not to store the saw under tension.

Never force the saw when cutting, and take extra care when starting the cut – saw more gently at first until the saw blade is established in the groove created.

UNDERSTANDING
Handsaws

It is useful to have a variety of handsaws at your disposal to tackle the range of shapes and thicknesses of material you may have to saw. The blade size, as well as the size, number, and shape of the teeth, will determine a saw's best uses.

Hacksaw

Jacksaw

244

66 HOWEVER MUCH FORCE YOU PUT IN, SAWING STEADY AND STRAIGHT IS ALWAYS FASTEST! **99**

Japanese pull saw (Ryoba)

Folding arborist's saw

Hacksaw

■ **Fine-toothed blade** With its metal frame and fine-toothed blade, a hacksaw is used for cutting small bits of metal, such as threaded bars or bandsaw blades.

■ **Not key to woodcraft** Not very useful for the woodworker, generally.

Jacksaw

■ **Multi-purpose** As the name suggest, a multi-purpose tool, useful for both crosscutting and ripping.

■ **Choose large teeth** For sawing green wood choose a saw with large teeth (such as 7tpi), since they do not clog up with waste wood as readily as smaller-toothed blades.

■ **Cuts on the push stroke** Be careful not to allow the blade to buckle.

■ **Aim for steady, straight cuts** Think of your forearm as only moving in one place, then line up your body to put some extra strength into the action.

Japanese pull saw

■ **A multipurpose carpentry saw** This saw has two cutting edges, one for ripping and one for crosscutting.

■ **Great for cutting joints** Also good for general-purpose sawing, giving a neater surface on the cut.

■ **Reinforced spine** You can also buy saws with reinforced spines – the spine can cause the saw to get stuck on larger bits of wood or boards, but it does hold it straight for accuracy when sawing tenons, for instance.

Folding arborist's saw

■ **Perfect for green woodworking** They are designed for arborists who work mostly with wet wood.

■ **Very efficient at cutting** This saw cuts through wood efficiently, and is available in a variety of sizes.

■ **Convenient for carrying** They are of a useful design for carrying and storing, as they come in their own ready-made sheath – this one is a great size for stuffing into a small pack.

Safety Tips

Secure the wood being sawn with clamps, to stop it moving around as you cut.

Store saws in protective sleeves, both to protect the blade and to avoid causing injuries.

Beware the saw jumping out of the cut: keep your hand out of harm's way.

Plan for the bit of wood that you are cutting off, especially if it is a large log.

There are a large number of different types of drill bits, each one suited to a specific purpose. Battery-powered drills are very useful, particularly for small holes and for speed, but the traditional tools are still best for certain jobs: for depth accuracy you can't beat counting the turns of a brace and bit.

Brace

"T" auger

BRACE

■ **Chuck jaws** The brace has V-shaped blocks to clamp on to the tapered shank of bits. Modern braces can have different chucks: make sure the bits you use match the chuck on the brace or drill.

■ **Rounded handle** The handle can be braced against your body to add stability. If the lead screws are good then the bit should draw itself through the wood without much force from behind.

AUGER

■ **Nickers cut a clean hole** An auger is a useful tool for drilling larger holes – though some claim the nicker can drag across the end grain and distort the hole into an oval.

■ **Bullnose auger** Shown here, the bullnose auger cuts extremely well and is useful for drilling into end grain, as well as widening holes and drilling into wood at an angle.

■ **Large augers** Know as "T" or eye augers, large augers enable a lot of power and allow you to get your body in a good position.

■ **Scotch pattern** These are the most common "T" augers. They don't have a nicker and are easy to sharpen with a triangular file; *see* p180.

SHARPEN

Do not sharpen the outside of augers and drill bits, as this will change the shape and size of the hole the tool cuts.

The Geometry

The "lip", or "cutter", of the auger should be kept sharp. If there is a raised spur on the very end of the cutting lip – sometimes known as a "nicker" – it should also be sharpened. If damaged, the lead screw can be restored with a needle file or small triangular file.

Nicker *should be filed from the inner face*

Lead screw

Lip *should be filed from below*

AUGER BIT

The Process

1 File the cutting edges
A diamond file is a good choice for achieving a polished cutting edge on an auger or drill bit. For some bits a small triangular file may be best.

2 Use a round file on concave surfaces
If sharpening concave sections of an auger or drill bit – such as the inside of the end of a bullnose auger – use a round file.

3 Use a grinding wheel
A simple metal twist drill bit is best sharpened on a grinding wheel.

Safety Tips

▶ **Wear protective gear** including safety goggles.

▶ **Do not touch the bit** after using an electric drill – it will be hot.

DRILL BITS

■ **Auger bit** This bit cuts cleanly, and can be used in a brace: if the lead screw is good you can achieve very accurate depths by counting the number of turns of the brace.

■ **Extenders increase accuracy** An extender increases the distance between hole and drill, which helps with sighting, increasing accuracy, and for lining up holes over distances.

■ **Other specialist bits** Bits specially designed for cutting wood (including flat bits), for cutting metal, and for use in masonry are available. Flat bits are less useful for tough woods; metal twist drill bits work fine for small holes in wood.

Auger bit with extender

Extra long auger bit

Masonry bit

Lip and spur bit

Metal-drilling bit

Flat bit

Bit for a brace

Measuring Tools

Along with the standard long metal ruler and sharp pencil, there are a number of highly useful measuring tools that should be part of a woodworker's arsenal. Accurate measuring is the foundation of joinery. Take good care of your measuring tools – and double-check everything!

**Adjustable
pointed arms**
*allow for easy
measuring*

Dividers

CM

Calipers

Vernier calipers

Two sets of jaws
for measuring internal and external diameters

CALIPERS

■ **Used to measure diameters**; this style is employed specifically for external diameters, but others are designed to measure internal diameters, sometimes both.

■ **Check measurements quickly** by simply setting the calipers to the diameter of the object being measured, then holding them against a ruler (or vice versa).

■ **Useful for checking** diameters when turning spindles or bowls on a lathe.

DIVIDERS

■ **As the name suggests**, these can be very useful for dividing up spaces, particularly when divisions needed are not on a straight line.

■ **Quickly and efficiently** mark with the pointed ends, which can stay put as you swivel the dividers around, meaning there is less chance of error.

■ **Good for scoring curves** into boards or blanks, when used like a pair of compasses.

■ **Measure distance on awkward** three-dimensional objects, such as that between the base of a chair's seat and a specific part of one of its legs.

VERNIER CALIPERS

■ **Useful for transferring measurements**, just like other calipers, but with in-built calibration and the benefit of increased accuracy thanks to the Vernier scale.

■ **Internal and external jaws** can both be used to measure widths and thicknesses, and the stem can also be used to measure depths – particularly useful for measuring the depths of drilled holes.

■ **Jaws can be locked** to further reduce the chance of mistakes while transferring measurements.

Cutting disc *tries to drag away from the fence, keeping it tight and accurate*

Marking knife

Marking gauge

Stock or fence *rubs along datum surface*

Try square

MARKING KNIFE

■ **Align against a ruler** and use instead of a pencil for effective, accurate marking out – the sharp point is more precise; fill in the line with pencil for clarity.

■ **Transfer measurements quickly,** for instance when making dovetail pins straight from the tails.

■ **Asymmetric grind** causes the blade to be drawn towards the datum, which is beneficial for accuracy.

MARKING GAUGE

■ **Scribes an accurate line** from a given datum surface, which can then be drawn in with a pencil or cut with a knife – but remember that this line will only be as accurate as the datum it was measured from.

■ **Adjustable stock** can measure a range of distances.

■ **The wheel scores** the line. Other variations, such as those that score with a pin or knife, are available, but the wheel works particularly well running along the grain as it tends not to follow the fibres as much as other types. The shape of the disc draws it away from the stock, holding the stock firmly against the work piece.

Sliding bevel

SLIDING BEVEL

■ **Adjustable arm** enables tool to measure any angle.

■ **Locking screw** keeps the angle in place, and is located in an unobstrusive place on this Japanese model.

■ **A sliding bevel** can be used just like a try square.

TRY SQUARE

■ **There are two parts**: the stock and the blade. This one has a wooden stock with a brass face plate to keep it true. It is designed to be used on solid three-dimensional objects: the stock rests against a datum surface and the blade is used to cut or draw a line at 90° to it.

■ **Three brass bolts** hold the two pieces together.

■ **Test for trueness** by lining the try square up with a known straight edge and drawing a square line on it, then flip the try square and draw another line – if the square is accurate, the two lines should be parallel.

HOW TO

SHARPEN

The marking knife must have a flat side so that it can sit accurately against the rule or square. Orienting the bevel this way guides it towards the rule, making sure that it doesn't get dragged off course by the grain.

The Geometry

A Japanese marking knife with a forged hollow on the inside makes it quick to flatten when sharpening. It is important that one side of the blade is flat, as it should rest against the side of a ruler when you are measuring and marking out.

Bevel side

Marking knife *should have a 25° edge angle*

Hollow ground *surface*

Hollow side

The Process

Grind one side of a marking knife flat

A marking knife needs to have one side perfectly flat, to ensure accurate measurements. A diamond stone is a good choice of abrasive to achieve this.

Sharpen the disc of a marking gauge

If your marking gauge has a wheel, unscrew the disc and rub it on a diamond stone, or any other flat abrasive, to sharpen it.

File the points of dividers

Use a fine file or stone to sharpen the two points of dividers, as it is useful for the ends to be sharp.

CHAPTER 05

HARDWARE

Nothing is more satisfying than creating your own wood crafting hardware from scratch. Tailor-make your equipment to suit your needs and take your craft to the next level.

MAKE A
SHAVING HORSE

A shaving horse is effectively a work bench, clamp, and seat combined into a single piece of hardware, adapted for efficient working with a draw knife: the harder you pull, the stronger the clamping force from your legs.

YOU WILL NEED

TOOLS & EQUIPMENT

- Pencil, marking knife, and measuring equipment
- Axe and axe block
- 16mm (⅝in) tenon cutter
- Straight knife
- Sliding bevel
- Electric drill with 16mm (⅝in) bit and 16mm (⅝in) reamer
- Frame saw and pull saw
- Mortise chisel and mallet
- Hammer and safety goggles

MATERIALS

- For the legs: 4 x billets of green wood, trued to around 60mm (2⅜in) x 508mm (20in)
- For other pieces: scaffolding planks, 3m x 225 x 36mm (3ft 10in x 8⅞ x 1⁷⁄₁₆in), sawn into sections indicated below
- For pegs: 1 green wood log, about 60mm (2⅜in) diameter and 260mm (10¼in) long
- For the arm pin: mild steel rod, 9mm (⅜in) wide and 330mm (13in) long
- Bolts and washers
- 80mm (3⅛in) wood screws
- PVA glue and swizzle stick

SKILLS

REMIND YOURSELF HOW TO

- Shape with an axe: *p50*
- Form a tapered tenon: *pp56, 130*
- Use a tenon cutter: *p130*
- Use a reamer: *p130*
- Use a chisel: *p118*
- Peg joints: *p130*
- Level legs: *p154*

KNIFE GRIPS

- Chest lever: *p19*
- Thumb push: *p22*
- Shin pull: *p63*
- Thumb pull: *p21*

DESIGN GUIDE

Based on a traditional "dumbhead" style, we have kept this design very simple and cheap. To use it, you push the treadle forwards with your feet to bring the swinging arm down towards the platform, thereby clamping the billet with the head. Longer billets can be placed along either side of the arm, and the angled platform enables efficient shaving action.

HEAD PIECES: 152 x 114mm (6 x 4½in)

SWINGING ARM: 762 x 114mm (30 x 4½in)

Swinging arm *fitted to platform by metal pin*

PLATFORM: 762 x 222mm (30 x 8¾in)

PLATFORM SUPPORT: 222 x 165mm (8¾ x 6½in)

BENCH: 1372 x 222mm (54 x 8¾in)

Splayed legs *and tapered tenon joints provide strength and stability*

TREADLE: 406 x 114mm (16 x 4½in)

Treadle attached *to swinging arm by a wooden peg*

3D VIEW

" A HORSE MAKES IT **INGENIOUSLY** SIMPLE AND QUICK TO **ROTATE** AND **FLIP** A WORK PIECE. "

TIP

Hold the leg at the angle of taper, then axe straight down towards the block. The long length helps with accuracy.

" A TENON CUTTER IS IN ESSENCE JUST A LARGE PENCIL SHARPENER. "

The Process

1 Rough taper the leg tenons

Using an axe, cut a tapered tenon on each leg piece. Draw a circle slightly larger than the thin end of the tenon, in the centre at one end; you could draw round a small coin. Start the taper quite far down the leg and chop angled facets all round; *see* Tip, above. Cut a square around the circle mark, then take off the corners with finer cuts until it is roughly circular.

Techniques: Shaping with an axe, forming a tapered tenon – see pp50, 56

Blend in *the shoulder until smooth and even*

2 Finish the tapers

Test fit the tenon cutter: any areas where it isn't fitting will show with scuff marks. Shave these down with a knife in chest lever grip. Once it fits, twist the tenon cutter round the end to create a perfect taper, making sure the tenon stays centred. If the cutter creates a shoulder, remove it with a knife in thumb push grip.

Technique: Using a tenon cutter – see p130

Knife grip: Chest lever, thumb push – see pp19, 22

ANGLING THE REAMER

Remember to account for the reamer's taper, either try to sight straight down the centre of the reamer, or adjust the sliding bevel so that you can sight the outside of the reamer, aligned with the sliding bevel.

For example, our reamer has a 6.4° taper (or 12.8° included angle, i.e. the angles on both sides of the reamer combined), so you need to adjust the sliding bevel by the same amount, adding 6.4° degrees to it.

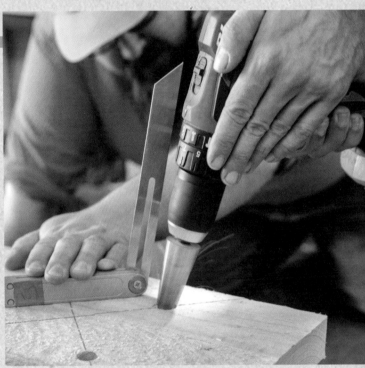

3 Drill the leg mortises

On what will be the underside of the platform, mark the mortise hole positions for the leg tenons, 127mm (5in) from the end and 51mm (2in) from the sides. Draw sight lines for each hole at 45° and set a sliding bevel to 15° for the angle of splay. With the section resting on axe blocks or a work bench, drill the holes right through. Get someone to help you sight it straight and at the correct angle, or use a mirror.

Place an offcut *underneath to avoid breakout*

4 Ream the leg mortises

Taper the mortises to match the leg tenons by drilling them with a reamer cutting attachment. Make sure you are drilling at the correct angle, ideally with some help sighting as you drill; *see* above. Drill to the full depth of the reamer so as to make the largest and strongest joint possible.

Technique: Using a reamer attachment – see p130

CONTINUED ☞

TIP
Scoring the pencil guidelines with a marking knife creates a groove to help the saw and chisel blades cut accurately.

5 Mark out slots for the swinging arm

Mark out slots for the swinging arm on the bench and platform sections. Draw a line down the middle of each, starting 279mm (11in) from one end for both sections, but extend the line to 356mm (14in) on the bench and only 305mm (12in) on the platform. Mark the width of the slots, centred on these lines and equivalent to the thickness of the plank with 1mm (¹⁄₃₂in) leeway either side. Go over the lines with a marking knife to score in the edges.

6 Saw the long edges

Drill access holes in each corner of one end of a slot, wide enough to fit a frame saw blade. Insert the blade, make sure it's correctly angled and fixed, then saw straight down a long edge. Swap sides and repeat. If using a turning saw then turn it to take the short cut between the two long ones; if you can't with the saw you could use a chisel.

7 Chisel the ends

Chisel out a section at one of the short ends of the slot. Hold the chisel perpendicular and hit the end of the handle with a mallet to cut out a chip, then tilt the chisel to lever out the chip. Repeat to cut across the width of the slot. Chip out another section, then remove further layers, progressively deeper, until you cut right through. Repeat at the opposite end until the slot falls out, then tidy up any ragged edges with the chisel. Repeat for the other slot.

Technique: Using a chisel – see p118

Chipping out *a second section gives clearance to the blade*

8 Form the platform support

Take the platform support piece and, in the centre at one end, mark and saw out a tenon 80mm (3⅛in) wide (about one-third of the width of the plank) and as long as the platform thickness. If the support has any cupping it is worth removing this with a plane before marking out the mortise. Hold the tenon against the platform to mark a corresponding mortise, starting 60mm (2⅜in) from the end of the platform, then line the tenon up to it and draw round. Score the guidelines with a marking knife and chisel out the slot as described in step 7.

CONTINUED ☞

TIP
The wood of a scaffold plank is soft, so gluing the legs helps to harden the wood around the joints.

9 Cut the treadle slot

Mark the slot in the treadle for the arm by drawing a centre line, marking a point 203mm (8in) from one end, placing the swinging arm vertically centred at this point, and then drawing round it to set the width. Saw along these lines, then chisel it out as in step 7.

Hold the treadle
secure on a block or other work surface, as you saw

10 Fit a leg

Spread glue around the inside of a leg mortise with a swizzle stick or wood shaving, then bang in the leg. Draw a line across the side of the bench at the angle of splay, centred along the tenon. Mark a point just under halfway up this line, so there is plenty of tenon to drill into and enough of the body plank for strength. Drill a 10mm (⅜in) hole, straight on all planes and to the full length of the bit, through the bench and leg tenon.

Cleave out two billets from a quartersawn section of the log and rough shape them with an axe to around 20mm (13⁄16in) square.

Holding the billet in the middle, use a knife in shin pull grip to first round one side to 10mm (3⁄8in), then taper its end to 8mm (5⁄16in).

Repeat on the other side and saw the billet in two. Finally, use thumb pull grip to chamfer the wider ends, to protect them from splitting when they are hammered.

11 Peg the leg

Draw a pencil line on a peg to the depth of the hole just drilled and spread glue around the thinner end. Insert the peg by hand, then knock it in with a hammer until the pencil line is buried in the hole; the sound of the hammer should change pitch once it is all the way in. Saw off the peg waste. Repeat for the other legs and adjust their heights so that the horse sits level at around 500mm (19 11⁄16in) from the top of the seat to the floor.

Techniques: Pegging joints, levelling legs – see pp130, 154

12 Peg the treadle and arm

Place the arm into the treadle slot with the treadle ever so slightly angled, as in the photo of the finished horse; you are aiming to drill through the centre of the arm around 76mm (3in) from the bottom. Drill a 12mm (1⁄2in) hole through one side of the treadle, enough to mark the arm, then take them apart and continue drilling both separately, so that you can push a peg through the arm and both sides of the treadle.

Leave the peg *proud so that the treadle position can be adjusted*

CONTINUED ☞

13 Drill the head pieces

Place a head piece 25mm (1in) from the top of the swinging arm and draw a guideline along its top edge. Mark positions on the head piece for the three bolt holes: two 25mm (1in) in from the corners of a short edge, the third between these two and then 89mm (3½in) from the rear edge (*see* right). Drill holes right through both head pieces using a drill bit the same diameter as your bolts.

14 Bolt head to the arm and bend the pin

Place a head piece back on the arm, lined up with the guideline drawn in step 13. Insert the drill through the holes and use it to mark the bolt hole positions on the arm. Remove the head and drill holes all the way through the arm, then bolt the head pieces tightly into position. For added strength you could glue them, but you may need to replace the head from time to time, so the bolts bring flexibility. Put on safety googles to hammer one end of the metal pin against the edge of an axe block, to form a bent handle.

Make sure
*the screws do
not sit proud*

15 Fit the metal pin

Drill 10mm (⅜in) holes for the metal pin through the centre of the side of the platform, 254mm (10in) from the mortise end. It is vital to drill straight, so draw guidelines and drill in two stages: first with a thinner bit through to the slot, marking the hole on the other side; then with the correct size drill bit all the way through. Drill a corresponding hole in the arm, 25mm (1in) from the front edge and 114mm (4½in) from the base of the head. For extra flexibility, it is worth drilling a series of holes for the pin in the arm, around 51mm (2in) apart, and additional holes on the platform as well.

16 Screw the platform to the bench

Attach the platform to the bench with a pair of screws at the non-raised end, then further secure by drilling two more screws from underneath the bench up into the platform support.

MAKE A

WORK BENCH & POLE LATHE

This easy-to-construct work bench will provide a solid, stable surface for carrying out tasks such as sawing, drilling, and hammering. And if you decide to try your hand at wood turning, the bench provides a platform around which to construct a pole lathe.

YOU WILL NEED

TOOLS & EQUIPMENT

■ Pencil, long ruler, try square, sliding bevel, protractor, and spirit level

■ Handsaws (including a pull saw)

■ Electric drill with drill bits, including 30mm (1³⁄₁₆in) flat wood bit

■ Hacksaw

■ Metal file

■ Mortise chisel and small mallet

■ Draw knife and shaving horse

■ Mallet, froe, and wedges

■ Axe and axe block

■ Chalk line

■ F-clamps

■ Scrub plane

■ 25mm (1in) auger

■ 2 x wrenches or spanners

■ Straight knife

■ *optional*: Bench stop, metal crank, brace

MATERIALS

■ For the bench: 4 x 3m (9ft 10in) lengths of planed "2 x 4" planks

■ For the bench legs: 4 x billets split from a green wood log and shaped to around 1016mm (40in) long and 102mm (4in) wide, left to dry completely

■ For the treadle: 1 green wood log, around 270mm (10⅝in) in diameter, and at least 1130mm (44½in) long

■ For the poppets: 1 green wood log, around 279mm (11in) in diameter and 660mm (26in) long

■ For the tool rest: 1 dry plank, 775 x 55 x 30mm (30½ x 2³⁄₁₆ x 1³⁄₁₆in)

■ For the wedges: 2 dry planks, 406 x 23 x 95mm (16 x ⅞ x 3¾in)

■ For the arms: 2 dry planks, 1600 x 102 x 51mm (63 x 4 x 2in), edges taken off

■ 2 dry wooden pegs, 14mm (⁹⁄₁₆in) in diameter and 152mm (6in) long

■ Bungee cord, around 4.1m (13ft 5in) long

■ Starter cord for motors, around 2.7m (9ft) long

■ M8 (8mm/⁵⁄₁₆in) threaded steel rod, enough for four sections just less than 356mm (14in) long, for the bench, and two sections 90mm (3½in) long, for the turning centres of the lathe

■ 8 x 30mm (1³⁄₁₆in) washers

■ 8 x 8mm (⁵⁄₁₆in) nuts, 4 x 10mm (⅜in) nuts

■ 5 x 10mm (⅜in) nuts and bolts for treadle

■ PVA glue

■ *optional*: Sheet of stiff plastic, for dovetail template

SKILLS

YOU WILL LEARN TO

■ Form countersink holes with a drill: *step 2*

■ Form a sliding dovetail joint: *steps 6–14*

■ Use a chalk line: *step 18*

REMIND YOURSELF HOW TO

■ Use an electric drill: *p24*

■ Use a pull saw: *p24*

■ Use a chisel: *p118*

■ Use a draw knife: *p94*

■ Level legs: *p154*

■ Split with a froe: *p82*

■ Shape with an axe: *p50*

■ Use a plane: *p100*

■ Use an auger: *p30*

KNIFE GRIP

■ Thumb pivot: *p22*

“ THE **LEGS** FIT BY **SLIDING DOVETAIL JOINTS**, WHICH MAY LOOK TRICKY, BUT WITH THE **AID** OF **TEMPLATES** ARE IN FACT FAIRLY **SIMPLE TO ACHIEVE.** ”

Design guide

By inserting poppets and arms, and wedging the arms taut with a crossbar, if necessary, the bench is quickly converted into a lathe. To use the lathe, loop the bungee around the arms, resting it on the pegs, and tie off with a knot, adjusting to get the right tension. Tie one end of the treadle cord at the widest point of the swinging arm, wrap it around the arm and thread through the notch at the end, then tie the other end to the bungee; once the cord is wrapped around the billet for turning, adjust its length to get the correct tension by looping or unlooping it around the arm.

CROSSBAR

BUNGEE

PEG

Flexible bungee *retracts string after each pull*

SUPPORTING ARM

1600 mm (63in)

STRING

String is pulled *up and down by treadle, causing billet to spin*

BILLET TO BE TURNED

POPPET

Supporting arms *slot into bench via mortise-and-tenon joints*

TURNING CENTRES

TOOL REST

SLIDING DOVETAIL JOINT

BENCH PLANKS

THREADED BAR

WEDGE

Poppets fit into *central bench slot, which can also be used to saw into*

1016 mm (40in)

TREADLE

Treadle worked *by foot to pull on the string*

Wedge the treadle *legs against a wall or dig into the ground*

WORK BENCH AS POLE LATHE, 3D VIEW

TURNING CENTRE:
40mm (1⁹⁄₁₆in) from
top and 25mm (1in)
from tool rest side

95mm
(3¾in)

178mm (7in)

610mm (24in)

250mm (9¹³⁄₁₆in)

WEDGE SLOT:
25mm (1in) wide

76mm
(3in)

178mm (7in)

POPPET SIDE VIEW
with front view of slot

Arm pivots *so that
the string can be
directed to either
side of the billet*

SWINGING ARM:
1105 x 76 x 51mm
(43½ x 3 x 2in)

PIVOT PIECE:
273 x 64mm
(10¾ x 2½in)

widest point:
76mm (3in)

457mm (18in)

FOOT REST: 457 x
76mm (18 x 3in)

LEGS: 889 x 64mm
(35 x 2½in)

TREADLE, 3D VIEW

B

A

35 mm (1³⁄₈in)

D

C

64mm (2½in)

LARGE TAPERING SLIDING
DOVETAIL TEMPLATE
(actual size)

B

A

25mm (1in)

D

C

40mm (1⁹⁄₁₆in)

SMALL TAPERING SLIDING
DOVETAIL TEMPLATE
(actual size)

TIP

Hold the planks steady on a suitable work surface; straddling two axe blocks allows you to saw into the gap between.

The Process

Check the depth
of the countersink hole with a ruler

1 Saw planks to length

Use a handsaw to cut three of the "2x4" planks in half, to give you six 1.45m (4ft 9in) lengths. Mark accurate lines with a ruler, pencil, and try square before sawing, and cut with a diagonal action. Saw two shorter pieces 305mm (12in) long from the remaining plank; these will form the mid-section of the work bench, creating a slot for sawing into and which also accommodates the pole lathe poppets.

2 Countersink holes for the nuts

Mark two crosses on one of the wide faces of a plank: the first at 110mm (4⁵⁄₁₆in) from the end and 35mm (1³⁄₈in) in from the edge; the second 225mm (8⁷⁄₈in) from the end and 35mm (1³⁄₈in) in from the opposite edge. Cut holes at the crosses with the flat wood drill bit to a depth of 10mm (³⁄₈in). Repeat at the other end to cut mirror image holes, then cut matching holes in a second plank.

Technique: Using an electric drill
– see p24

Place a nut *on the bar for a guiding edge as you saw*

3 Drill through the planks

Mark the centre of each countersink hole and drill right through the plank at these points, using the 10mm (⅜in) bit. Measure and mark crosses at the corresponding points on all the other planks, including at one end of each of the two shorter ones, and drill holes through at these points as well. It is vital that all the holes match up and are drilled straight, since even a small misalignment will prevent the bar threading all the way through the planks; using a drill bit with a slightly wider diameter than the rods provides some leeway.

4 Size the bar and file the ends

Cut the threaded bars slightly undersize, by 10mm (⅜in) less than the combined thickness of the planks, since the final width of the bench will be narrower when the wood is compressed. Saw it off with a hacksaw in four equal lengths. Use a metal file to take the thread off the last 3mm (⅛in) at either end of each piece, and remove any sharp edges at the tips (*see* left).

CONTINUED ☞

TIP
Always check that the components align before gluing them down.

File down
the ends of any bars that sit proud

5 Build up the bench
Fit a washer and nut on the end of each bar and insert them through the drilled holes of one of the countersunk planks. Turn the plank over so the bars point upwards, spread PVA glue down its length, and slot the next plank on top. Repeat for the remaining planks, fitting the shorter planks after the third long plank and remembering not to glue where the wood is exposed in the slot. Finish with the second countersunk plank and attach the washers and nuts.

6 Begin the leg mortises
First mark a line along the upper surface of the bench, 200mm (7⅞in) from one end. Place the larger dovetail template on the upper surface, with point B on the 200mm (7⅞in) line and side AB along the edge of the bench, and draw round it. Turn the bench on its side and extend a line from point B over the side, at an angle of 107° measured from the edge of the bench. On the underside of the bench, draw round the large template, aligning point A with the line just drawn.

" IT IS VERY IMPORTANT THAT THE LEGS SPLAY OUT, SINCE THIS GIVES THE WORK BENCH ALL-IMPORTANT STABILITY. "

TIP
Saw towards the centre from both sides in turn – it's easier to get the joint looking neat this way.

7 Mark the small template

Flip the bench back over and place the smaller template over the first, with point D of each aligned. Draw round it, then extend line AC to the edge of the bench, and continue the line over the side to meet point B of the large trapezium on the base. This shape will form a strong, sliding dovetail joint. Now mark out all four mortises, remembering that opposing and adjacent pairs of joints should be mirror images of each other.

Make sure *the lines don't intersect with the bolts*

8 Saw down the sides

Use a pull saw to saw as accurately as you can down the sides of the mortise. Keep an eye on the alignment of the saw: you should be cutting along all three pencil lines on each face. Start sawing diagonally at a corner, then slowly angle the saw forwards as you cut, so you end up sawing straight down. Stop exactly on the line at the base of the trapeziums. Saw down the other side.

Technique: Using a pull saw – see p24

Aim to saw *precisely along the pencil lines*

CONTINUED ☞

Take care *not to chisel beyond the saw cuts*

Keep an eye out *for knots, which can damage your chisel*

Approach from above *and sides, but do not take material off the sides themselves*

9 Chop out the mortise

Starting at the thin end of the mortise, use a chisel and mallet to chop out small sections of wood. A sliding dovetail is designed to jam material in, hence it is not always easy to chisel wood out. Line up the edge of the chisel with the pencil lines at the sides of the mortise. Tap down with the mallet until chips start to come out. Move down 10mm (⅜in) at a time with the chisel, then come around the other side of the mortise.

Technique: Using a chisel – see p118

10 Pare down

When you get close to the base of the mortise, switch to paring rather than chipping out. Hold the chisel with both hands, one low down and one near the top, supporting it against your chest. If using a square chisel, take great care at the corners of the mortise, which are at tighter angles than the points of the chisel. Repeat steps 8–10 for the other mortises.

TIP

Skewing the leg end before using the template adjusts the effective angles the template will create, making them more accurate.

11 Begin leg tenon

Hold a leg against a mortise, so that the top of the leg is level with the top of the bench. Tilt the leg in turn to the angle of splay in both planes of the mortise, and draw corresponding lines on the leg to indicate the sloping section to be removed from the top. Saw this off, leaving an angled top. Place the large template on this sawn end and draw round it.

A stiff plastic *template gives a good edge to draw round*

12 Shape the dovetail

On your shaving horse, use a draw knife to shape the leg tenon to the template. Start with the CD side of the trapezium, which will sit along the bottom face of the mortise, then cut AC and BD, before finishing with AB. Create parallel lines running down the leg from the four points of the trapezium, with flat faces between them. The tenon must be long enough to fit all the way into the mortise, so make your parallel lines extend around 50mm (2in) further than the length of the mortise.

Technique: Using a draw knife – see p94

Check the width *down the leg with the large template*

CONTINUED ☞

> 66 BY **TAPERING** THE TENON TO **ONE SIDE** WE GAIN AS MUCH **SPLAY** AS POSSIBLE: **AROUND 20°**. 99

Make sure that *all the faces of the leg are flat*

13 Taper the tenon

Place the small template on the end of the tenon, with point B of each trapezium aligned, and draw round it. You now need to shave an even taper down from the limit of the tenon to this new guideline; or in other words from the large trapezium down to the shape of the small trapezium at the tip of the tenon. The tenon must fit as tightly as possible at its limit, so do not make the taper longer than it needs to be. We are relying on the taper along the length of the tenon to create some of the splay, which makes cutting the mortise simpler as it can be straight backed.

14 Refine the tenon fit

Sharp corners can dig into the mortise and cause problems, so cut a thin chamfer off the edges of the tenon before fitting it. When testing the fit, make sure the back is aligned flat and adjust the sides as needed. All of the faces need to be flat; any roundness will create a pivot point, and there will not be enough surface contact between the mortise and tenon for a strong leg.

TIP

If one of the treadle billets has a curve to it, choose this for the swinging arm, which needs a slight curve anyway.

15 Assemble

Repeat for the other legs, checking they splay in the correct direction. Fit and level the legs, and saw off any protruding sections of tenon. Finally, drill holes along the centre of the bench for bench stops and hold fasts. These are commonly 18.5mm (¾in) in diameter and set 51mm (2in) apart, but check the size of your hardware; you may prefer to drill as and when needed.

Technique: Levelling legs – see p154

Use a try square *to help drill straight*

16 Split out treadle billets

Take the treadle log and split out billets for the five pieces. Using a mallet, froe, and wedges, split the log in half, then into quarters down the radius, then split along the radius again to form wedges 70mm (2¾in) at their fattest point. Split these wedges in half again, but this time tangentially to leave triangular and quadrilateral wedges. Select the billets and saw them to length; avoid using the triangular billets from the centre of the wood for longer pieces, as these tend to be more twisty and knotty.

Technique: Splitting with a froe – see p82

CONTINUED ☛

USING A CHALK LINE

1.

2.

A chalk line is a retractable length of string hel[d in]
a box filled with coloured chalk, and is a great too[l for]
marking straight lines over uneven timber surface[s.]

1. Secure both ends of the chalk line and hold [the]
string taut over where you want to mark a guideli[ne.]

2. Snap the string against the surface of the bl[ank]
to leave a coloured chalk line. Here, the chalk line
marks a centre line to guide the shaping, but it ca[n]
also be used to mark cutting edges.

Straighter sides make the pieces much easier to bolt

17 Shape the legs, foot rest, and pivot

Take a quadrilateral wedge and form a leg piece for the treadle. Mark guide points indicating the width plus 15 per cent shrinkage, and chop out waste to these markers with an axe. Switch to the shaving horse and use a draw knife to take off the bark and shave to a more evenly rectangular cross-section, with roughly straight edges. Repeat with the other leg, foot rest, and pivot cross-piece.

Technique: Shaping with an axe – see p50

18 Rough shape the arm

The swinging arm needs more careful shaping, so that it tapers at both ends and describes a gentle curve along its length. Make pencil marks indicating the width at either end, again allowing for shrinkage, then lay a chalk line down the centre; *see* above. Mark on the widest point of the arm, which needs to sit halfway between the foot rest and pivot, 457mm (18in) up from one end. Mark this with pencil guides and a chalk line. Follow these guides to axe the arm to size and at the same time shape a curved profile.

Highlight in pencil *where you need to shave to curve the end*

19 Hone the arm

Moving to the shaving horse, smooth off the axe cuts with a draw knife and accentuate the curve at the bottom end of the swinging arm. Cut a chamfer along all the edges of the rounded side and generally neaten. Don't go too thin at this stage, however, to allow for shrinkage. Leave all the treadle pieces to dry for around 2 weeks, then check the measurements and shave down further, if need be. Saw a notch centrally at what will be the top end of the swinging arm, 25mm (1in) deep and wide enough to hold the string securely.

20 Test the treadle fit

Drill 10mm (⅜in) holes for the bolts, at the points indicated on the design guide, using an electric drill. Do a dry run of bolting the pieces together and examining the treadle to see if there are any gaps between surfaces or if the swinging arm is being impeded in its movement. Make marks where any areas need shaving down (*see* right) and refine the fit on the shaving horse.

CONTINUED ☞

TIP
It can be helpful to approach from both ends in turn with the froe when splitting off a thin section such as this.

When truing sides, *the axe is good for efficiency, but the draw knife is best for accuracy*

21 Split out the poppets

With a mallet and froe, split the log for the poppets in half. Follow the sizing guide on p227 to draw guidelines for splitting off the corners and a section of the pith and first few annular rings, to create two blocks of wood that will become the pole lathe's poppets.

22 Shave the sides square

Place the billets you are working on your bench, and use bench stops, or blocks of wood held with F-clamps, to hold them in place. Shave one of the two thinner sides flat, to set a datum surface. Using a ruler and try square, mark out and square the opposite side, followed by the bark-free face, from that datum. Hold a ruler against each side to check they are flat.

Use a draw knife _to get the last little bits at the back_

23 Mark out the tenon

On the face opposite the bark side, measure and mark a centre line to the length of the poppet's tenon. Mark off the end of the tenon with a try square, then mark the thickness of the tenon with two more lines, either side of the centre line; these are your saw lines. Extend them carefully around the sides and top of the billet, then saw down the lines at the end of the tenon with a handsaw.

24 Shape the tenon

Use the mallet and froe to remove the sides of the tenon; they should come away easily since you have already sawn off the ends. Instead of trying to remove the whole side in one go, take off thin sections until just shy of the pencil line. Now clamp the billet on your bench, placing some spare bits of wood beneath the tenon to support it, and use a scrub plane, and then a draw knife, to smooth down the sides of the tenon, removing the last 2mm (1/16in) of wood so it is the right thickness to fit snugly into the bench.

Technique: Using planes – see p100

CONTINUED ☛

Flat sides *are important to give the wedge gripping surfaces*

> ❝ IT IS **VITAL** THAT THE **SIDES** OF THE **TOOL REST** ARE **PARALLEL** ALONG ITS **LENGTH.** ❞

25 Make the tool rest

Take the 775 x 55 x 30mm (30½ x 2³⁄₁₆ x 1³⁄₁₆in) plank and clamp it on your shaving horse. Use a draw knife to carefully round off one edge by chamfering it at a 45° angle, and then smoothing out the chamfer to a curve by gradually taking off the corners. Do one half first then turn the plank round to shape the other half.

26 Make wedges for the poppets

Take one of the two 406 x 23 x 95mm (16 x ⅞ x 3¾in) planks. Draw a straight line on one of the flat faces, sloping from a corner to a point 55mm (2³⁄₁₆in) from the far side. Remove most of the narrower section with an axe, then use the draw knife to shave down to the line. Round off the sloped side with the draw knife and chamfer the ends. Repeat with the other plank.

TIP

The wedges should poke out a little on either side, but not so much that you might bang your knee on one.

27 Mark wedge slots on the poppets

Place the poppets at either end of the work bench slot. Hold up a wedge underneath the bench, against the inside face of the poppet, with a small amount extending beyond the side of the bench. Draw a pencil line on the poppet to mark where the wedge comes down to. Remove the wedge and draw another pencil line on the poppet at the base of the bench. Remove the poppet and continue the lines around the face of the tenon; mark a centre line on the face, too.

Hold the chisel *vertically and tap it down*

28 Drill and chisel the slot

Place some spare wood underneath the tenon to hold it up, and clamp it to the bench. Using a 25mm (1in) auger, drill holes just shy of the two pencil marks you made; mark centrepoints for the auger by measuring 12.5mm (½in) in from each pencil line. For the lower hole, first drill straight down to bite into the wood, then bring the auger towards you to angle the hole inwards. Drill more straight holes between the first two to form the slot, then chisel off the peaks left by the auger at the sides of the slot. Repeat on the other poppet.

CONTINUED ☞

TIP
It is worth wedging in the poppets before marking out, to ensure they are in the correct position.

29 Mark out holes for the centres

Place the poppets back in the bench slot and wedge in, to mark out holes for the turning centres of the lathe. Measure and mark the centre point of the slot on one of the tenons, extending this point all the way up the centre of the inner face of the poppet. The hole should be 40mm (1⁹⁄₁₆in) down from the top of the poppet: measure and mark a horizontal line at this point. Form the points of the centres by filing down one end of each metal bar to a sharp point, forming a cone around 4mm (⅛in) long (*see* right).

30 Drill centre holes

Use a long 10mm (⅜in) drill bit to drill a hole through the poppet for the centre. Check you are drilling parallel to the bench with a spirit level, and sight down the slot to drill parallel to the sides of the poppet. To drill the second poppet, clamp it right next to the first and use the drilled hole as a guide: drill through the first poppet again, then into the second, and right through the other side. Place two 10mm (⅜in) nuts on the end of either centre, tighten them against each other with two wrenches, then screw them in tightly.

31 Mark lines for the tool rest platform

Wedge the poppets as far apart as they will go, whilst still being able to reach both with a ruler. Align the ruler with the centre points and draw lines along the side of each poppet. Measure 55mm (2³⁄₁₆in) – or the height of your tool rest – down from that point, and draw further lines. Mark a vertical line 25mm (1in) out from the centre on the inner face of each poppet, to give a wide platform for the tool rest.

32 Saw out the platform

Use a handsaw to saw down the pencil lines, starting with the horizontal line where the base of the tool rest will sit. Then, with the poppets wedged into the bench slot, saw down the vertical line to the point where the two lines meet. Remove the excess chunks of wood.

Technique: Using a pull saw – see p24

CONTINUED ☞

TIP

Arm holes must be far
enough from the bench end
to avoid splitting the wood,
but not too close to the
metal bars.

Ideally *get
someone to
sight the
angle*

33 Drill mortise holes for the arms

Draw a line 50mm
(1^{15}⁄$_{16}$in) from the end of the work
bench and mark a cross at the
midpoint for drilling the arm hole.
Set a sliding bevel to an angle of
14° and drill a hole all the way
through the bench at that angle,
using a 30mm (1³⁄₁₆in) wood-
cutting bit. Repeat to drill a hole
for the second arm at the opposite
end of the bench.

34 Shave cylindrical tenons on the arms

Back on the shaving horse, take
shavings off the bottom end of each arm to
form a smooth, cylindrical tenon. Start by
making a square shape, then take off the
corners to round it. For a snug fit, make
sure the tenons are not flared out in any
direction. Keep testing the fit and taking
off more wood if needed, until you can get
the first 25mm (1in) or so into the mortise
hole; then taper the rest of the tenon so it
is even. The tenons should go all the way
through the bench and sit a little proud
underneath it. Finish them by putting a
heavy chamfer on the ends, with a straight
knife held in thumb pivot grip.

35 Drill holes in the arms

Using a 14mm (⁹⁄₁₆in) auger or drill bit in your electric drill, or a brace if you have one, drill a hole at the centre of the top end of each arm. Make sure you drill far enough from the end to avoid splitting, but do not go too low, or there won't be enough space for you to stand under the string of the pole lathe; 90mm (3½in) from the end should be sufficient. Drill around 95 per cent of the way through – the lead screw should just poke out on the other side – then turn the plank over and finish drilling from the other side. This avoids tearout, giving you a neat hole.

36 Fashion pegs and an optional crossbar

Make non-tapering wooden pegs 14mm (⁹⁄₁₆in) long and tap them into the arm holes with a mallet; these are to hold up the bungee as the string pulls on it. Finally, make an optional crossbar to help strengthen the arms by sawing a roughly central V-notch at either end of the plank. You may first need to adjust the length of the plank, depending on the fit of the arms.

254
255

CONTRIBUTORS

ROBIN DUCKMANTON (CAPTAIN'S CHAIR)

Robin is a professional chair maker based in North Yorkshire. He has been a maker for 10 years, concentrating solely on chairs for the last five. He first learned frame chair making from Mike Abbott, then went to Tennessee to learn the art of American Colonial Windsor chair making from Curtis Buchanan. He makes and teaches from a wooden cabin at the end of his garden, using wood sourced from some of the highest-quality furniture making woodland in the UK.
redwoodchairs.co.uk
Instagram: @redwoodchairs

TOM HEPWORTH (BOWL)

Graduating from the prestigious Falmouth School of Art, Tom specialised in video editing before apprenticing with Barn the Spoon. He then helped establish The Green Wood Guild in London and now divides his time between making and teaching wood craft. His work is focussed on producing beautiful household items as "functional sculpture", grounded in traditional heritage crafts.

SOPHIE RIDLEY (FRAME STOOL)

Born and raised in Leeds, Sophie went on to complete a BA in Fine Art at Central Saint Martins. While studying, she explored interests in environmental art, collective practice, and more traditional craft. Since graduating, Sophie has remained in London, working in museums and galleries while also training in furniture design and art therapy with Barn the Spoon.

HARRY SAMUEL (TURNING)

After training at The Green Wood Guild and completing an apprenticeship at The Cherry Wood Project, Harry is now a full-time green wood craftsman and woodland worker based in the south west of the UK. He manages woodland to supply the raw materials for his work crafting treen, greenwood furniture, and timber frames.
Instagram: @sparry_hoons

TIM SANDERSON (JOINERY)

Tim gained a first class degree in Graphic Design at Kingston University London, where his fascination with materials and how things work led him to woodwork. Tim now teaches joinery and furniture making at The Green Wood Guild, and has a passion for turning bowls.

MORE ABOUT SPOONS

Spoonclub

Barn the Spoon set up his first Spoonclub with friends in 2010 as a place where people could get together to carve. There is now a growing number of clubs worldwide with a website where you can find your local club, buy tools and blanks, and subscribe to a large number of professionally produced video tutorials, which demonstrate everything from the real basics to advanced carving.

spoonclub.co.uk

SPŌN: A GUIDE TO SPOON CARVING AND THE NEW WOOD CULTURE (VIRGIN BOOKS, 2017)

Read more about spoon carving in this, Barn's first book, where he sets out his manifesto for making, and gives the reader a firm foundation in not just the techniques, but also the thinking behind the functional beauty of 16 different traditional styles of wooden spoon.

ACKNOWLEDGEMENTS

From the author

For the pulled fibre brush and chopping board inspiration:

JARROD DAHL FROM THE USA
Instagram: @woodspirithandcraft

For the coffee peg inspiration:

LEE SEIL FROM THE REPUBLIC OF KOREA
Instagram: @iseilnam

From the publisher

We would like to acknowledge the help of the following people in the production of this book: thanks to Louise Brigenshaw, Karen Constanti, Mandy Earey, and Simon Murrell for design assistance; Steve Crozier for repro work; Kathy Steer for editorial assistance; Marie Lorimer for indexing; and David Fisher, US consultant, for his work in ensuring that the technical details are correct for North American readers. Thanks also to Katie Abbott for kindly hosting us at her patch of woodland in Essex and providing such an inspirational day of green woodworking at the very start of the project.

Picture credits

The publisher would like to thank the following for their kind permission to reproduce their photograph:
9 Alamy Stock Photo: Miriam Heppell
All other images © Dorling Kindersley
For further information see: www.dkimages.com

> **66** BARNABY CARDER SPEAKS ABOUT SPOONS **MORE PASSIONATELY** THAN MOST PEOPLE SPEAK ABOUT ANYTHING. **99** – THE DAILY TELEGRAPH

ABOUT THE AUTHOR

BARN THE SPOON

Barnaby Carder opened his infamous London-based spoon shop in 2012 and his work popularising spoon carving has gained him much international acclaim. Barn's collaborations, such as Spoonfest and Spoonclub, have helped create the rise and rise in reputation of the humble wooden spoon. In *Wood Craft*, Barn builds on 20 years of craft and teaching, and his collaborations at The Green Wood Guild, to set out a project list with the aim of inspiring readers to get involved with wood craft and show them how.

Barn runs regular spoon carving workshops in London; to book a class or buy spoons head to: **barnthespoon.com**

THE GREEN WOOD GUILD

A little woodwork school founded in central London, The Green Wood Guild teaches wood craft to Londoners and the many international students it attracts. The Guild not only provides skilled teaching, but also respite for the city dwellers. People can come as a one-off to try out a short whittling workshop, but most then decide to complete the set of classes available, which include: bowl carving, furniture making, and knife forging. The Guild also provides information on the most appropriate local wood species to use and where to buy tools.
thegreenwoodguild.com

DISCLAIMER

Neither the author nor the publisher take any responsibility for any injury or damage resulting from the use of techniques shown or described in this book. The reader is advised to follow all safety instructions carefully, wear the correct protective clothing, and, where appropriate, follow all manufacturers' instructions.